A SOCIAL HISTORY
OF THE
POPULAR SEASIDE HOLIDAY

Beside the Seaside

James Walvin

ALLEN LANE

ALLEN LANE
Penguin Books Ltd
17 Grosvenor Gardens
London sw1w 0bd

First published in 1978

Copyright © James Walvin, 1978

isbn 0 7139 0744 4

Set in 11 point Monotype Bell
by Western Printing Services Ltd, Bristol
Printed in Great Britain by Billing & Sons Ltd,
Guildford, London and Worcester

List of Illustrations

The author and publishers are grateful to the following for permission to reproduce photographs: Blackpool District Central Library for nos. 5, 8; and the Metropolitan Borough of Sefton Libraries and Arts Services for nos. 15–18.

Acknowledgements

I am indebted to the staff of the following libraries: the Manchester Central Library, British Library, Southport and Blackpool Public Libraries, the Library of the Bognor Regis College of Education and New York Public Library. I was particularly helped by the collections – and the obliging staff – in the Scarborough Public Library and the Library of the Institute of Architectural Studies, University of York. Dr W. Sheils led me to the Rowntree Papers in the Borthwick Institute of Historical Research, but I owe my greatest debt to staff of the J. B. Morrell Library of the University of York.

Introduction

The English summertime rush to the sea is so customary, so fixed a part of the nation's annual routines, that it seems scarcely to require explanation; to tell English readers about the seaside is, in many respects, to tell them what they already know, for there must be few adults who do not have their own stories or memories of holidays and visits to the seaside. The recent history of the seaside is embedded in the individual and collective memories of the nation at large. There is, however, a more complex historical dimension to this story, and what follows is an attempt to describe the rise of the popular seaside holiday. It is a history which has been told many times before, best of all by J. A. R. Pimlott in *The Englishman's Holiday*, but that classic account is now thirty years old and in need of revision.

The story itself is quite remarkable. By 1900 millions of people had come to regard a visit to the seaside as a fact of urban life, yet a century before only the upper reaches of English society had been able – or even thought it worthwhile – to visit the seaside. To examine the history of the seaside holiday – to trace its progression from the preserve of the rich to becoming the annual treat of the urban working class – demands, not so much a study of resorts themselves but an investigation into the wider, shifting economic patterns of an advanced industrial society. The emergence of the popular seaside holiday provides a case study of those forces which enabled growing numbers of people to enjoy, and to regard as natural, those leisure pursuits towards which their forbears could only aspire. What follows is not a history of the resorts themselves, but an account of the social circumstances which transmuted them from small seaside villages into classic Victorian cities, catering for the varied leisure demands of urban people.

This book is written as an extended essay in social history which is both self-contained and yet a logical sequel to an earlier book, *The People's Game: A Social History of British Football*. And both books have been inspired by a determination to explore those historical forces which have helped to shape some of the most prominent characteristics of popular English leisure. Though not written for a scholarly audience, and lacking the apparatus which academics regard as vital, I trust that historical colleagues, no less than the general readership to whom it is directed, will find it acceptable. And it is to a most demanding, and stimulating, academic group – my fellow historians at the University of York – that I dedicate this book.

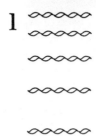

1   *Taking the Waters*

It goes without saying that the most obvious attraction of seaside towns is the sea itself, with its invigorating climate and breezes, coastline vistas and its sharp contrast to inland, urban life. And it was the sea which, in the early days of the maritime resorts, attracted the first trickles of upper-class visitors. But the physical and medicinal benefits of life by the sea – of strolling beside it, plunging into it and even drinking it – had for centuries been claimed for water of a very different kind. Throughout western Europe the inland spas – boasting a variety of natural and mineral waters – had long been what the seaside towns were to become: recreational centres where a minority could afford to refresh themselves, seek cures for their ailments and generally enjoy themselves at the variety of entertainments which the spas slowly evolved.

Across pre-industrial Europe, and even further afield, the sites of natural springs often developed into centres of social and religious activity and it is easy to see how places where the earth produced great freaks of nature – boiling water, steam or salt water inexplicably seeping from unyielding rock – should become the objects of human curiosity, superstitious customs, worship and cults. Gradually it came to be accepted that such waters often possessed medicinal benefits; but it was the expansion of imperial Rome and the entrenchment of Roman culture across Europe which helped to confirm the importance and to spread the custom of bathing in and drinking spring water. In England, the springs at Buxton and Bath are living reminders of Roman habits.

With the establishment of Christianity in western Europe, springs again became centres for worship and pilgrimage and by the Middle Ages commercial trade had often been spawned by the religious and temporal needs of the pilgrims. Although pilgrimages were rapidly curtailed by the forces of the English Reformation, so powerful had the cult of watering places become, that its survival was guaranteed, by folklore if by no other means. However, contemporary scientific evidence came to the rescue of the decaying spring-water towns with the first of what proved to be a spate of publications anxious to prove the curative powers of spring water. And it was to be a feature of spa and seaside towns, from the sixteenth century through to the early years of the twentieth, that local men of science could always be found to advocate the particular virtues of their own town's water.

This tradition began in 1562 when Dr William Turner published *A booke of the nature and properties of the bathes in England . . . Germany and Italy* in which he dealt, for the first time in English, with the subject of bathing. It is difficult to assess Turner's influence, though evidence suggests that the sick were visiting Bath and Buxton in the late sixteenth century. But the major expansion in spa towns did not occur until the seventeenth century – and then largely as a result of royal and upper-class patronage. The tendency, in the words of R. Lennard, was 'for the miracle-working holy wells of medieval England to become the medicinal springs of an age whose faith was in doctors rather than saints'.

For most seventeenth-century advocates of bathing, however, divine power was thought to work neatly in harmony with nature's benefits. 'Do not think the Baths can do you any good, without God's immediate Blessing on them, for it is God that must first *heal the Waters*, before they can have any virtue to heal you.' But the religious overtones of taking the waters inevitably declined as the spas became ever more prominent centres of secular leisure in Stuart England. No longer simply the Mecca for the sick, spas drew more and more upper-class visitors who cavorted through the spas' increasingly crowded season to the accompaniment of music, gambling and assignations. 'We pass our time awaye', wrote Sir Edmund Verney from Bath in August 1635, 'as merrily as paine will give us leave.'

The major spa towns, Harrogate, Tunbridge, Epsom,

Scarborough, Buxton, Bath and other smaller resorts, had become sophisticated centres of relaxation for those able to afford it. As the seventeenth century advanced, the vogue of taking the waters spread, with the consequent mushrooming of spas specifically designed to provide for the medicinal and social needs of those able – or desperate enough – to travel. In the years following the Restoration, the spas were sufficiently numerous to allow the English well-to-do to spend the entire summer season sampling their varied delights. Predictably, certain spas were dominant: Buxton, Harrogate and Scarborough in the north; Bath, Tunbridge, Epsom in the south. Only one, however, Scarborough – where spring waters were discovered in 1620 – was on the coast and it was to be a full century before changing medical opinion came to find in sea water the medicinal properties which were previously reserved for spa waters.

It was Bath which by the early eighteenth century exemplified the inland spa, its social respectability confirmed and enhanced by a visit of Queen Anne in 1702. To its matchless fashionable season of masques, balls, dinners and concerts there was slowly added the more substantial and lasting face of Georgian architecture which, to this day, remains an unequalled monument to the fashions of the age.

Polite society firmly believed in the apparent health-giving properties of spring-water bathing, more especially when it was accompanied by a fashionable round of social activity. Few shared Dr Johnson's scepticism: 'There is nothing in all this boasted system. No, sir; medicated baths can be no better than warm water: their only effect can be that of tepid moisture.' To the man who persisted in affirming the virtues of the baths, Dr Johnson tartly replied, 'Get thyself fumigated; but be sure that the steam be directed to thy *head*, for *that* is the *peccant part.*'

Inevitably, the spas provided cartoonists and caricaturists with a unique opportunity to display their severe graphic commentary. Fashionable society found itself mercilessly flayed in cartoon and sketch. And privately a number of prominent contemporaries deplored the spas' excesses. 'These watering-places,' wrote Walpole in 1766, 'that mimic a capital, and add vulgarities and familiarities of their own, seem to me like abigails in cast gowns.' Smollett's Squire Bramble was even more scathing:

> Every upstart of fortune, harnessed to the trappings of the mode, presents himself at Bath . . . Clerks and Factors from the East Indies, loaded with the spoil of plundered provinces; planters, negro-drivers and hucksters, from the American plantations, enriched they know not how; agents, commissaries, and contractors, who have fattened on two successive wars, on the blood of the nation; usurers, brokers, and jobbers of every kind; men of low birth and no breeding, have found themselves translated into a state of affluence, unknown to former ages . . . and all of them hurry to Bath, because here, without any further qualification, they can mingle with the princes and nobles of the land.

Yet in the years when Bath was enjoying its apogee of social fame, an obscure publication which was to revolutionize the practice of 'taking the waters' was receiving its first curious examination.

In 1750 Dr Richard Russell published a learned tract, *De Tabe Glandulari*, translated four years later as *A Dissertation concerning the Use of Sea-water in Diseases of the Glands*. This tract belonged to that long tradition of medical treatises written with a particular spa in mind. Indeed in the previous century the publications about the relative merits of mineral waters form a good illustration of the heightened curiosity in science at that time. Dr Russell, however, was unusual in claiming to have discovered in sea water the medicinal values traditionally associated with spa waters, although it is true that two previous authors – Dr Peter Shaw about 1730 and Sir John Floyer in 1734 – had praised the value of cold-water bathing. Russell was equally unusual in supporting his thesis by moving to the village of Brighthelmstone in Sussex to practise what he preached. Within a matter of years the newly named Brighton was to become a latter-day Bath; a social pace-setter for all seaside watering places.

Bathing in the sea did not of course begin with Russell's publication but had been a popular recreation for centuries. Joseph Strutt, in his book *Sport and Pastimes of the People of England*, published in 1802, wrote that 'swimming is an exercise of great antiquity; and no doubt familiar to the inhabitants of this country at all times. The heroes of the middle ages are sometimes praised for their skill in swimming.' It was thought to be among 'the requisites for a complete gentleman', and was particularly recommended 'to such as were inclined to follow a military profession'.

Nor was swimming restricted to seaside communities, and Strutt noted that 'boys in the country usually learn to swim with bundles of bull-rushes, and with corks where the rushes cannot be readily procured; particularly in the neighbourhood of London, where we are told, two centuries back, there were men who could teach the art of swimming well.'

Swimming was of course more commonplace by the seaside. In 1750, for example, Dr Pocock wrote that Exmouth was 'a place to which the people of Exeter much resort for diversion and bathing in the sea'. What Dr Russell did for seabathing was not to establish it, but to attract people to the coast from far afield. His thesis rapidly established itself as medical orthodoxy, its message purveyed through a number of legal and pirated editions. Advised and cautioned by their doctors, more and more of the wealthy began to transfer their loyalties from the inland spas to Brighton – and then to other small south-coast towns. There they behaved as they had traditionally done at the spas, by drinking and immersing themselves in the local water.

In Scarborough, 300 miles north, seabathing had already established itself as a fashionable recreation for well-to-do visitors, but the location and relative isolation of the town ensured that it remained ignored by southern society. Potentially, however, Scarborough could satisfy all tastes, for it boasted a unique combination of both spa and sea water and in the course of the seventeenth century the town had firmly established itself as a spa town, able to offer recreational diversions to that society whose natural centre of social gravity was York. Scarborough, like most spas, had its own medical protagonist in the form of Dr Robert Wittie, who argued as early as 1660 that the local spa water was 'good against diseases of the head, as the Apoplexy, Epilepsie, Catalepsie, Vertigo', and that it cured 'the jaunders both yellow and black, the leprosie . . . it is the Sovereign remedy against Hypochondriack Melancholly and Windiness.'

Long before Dr Russell's publication the accident of discovering spa water beside the sea at Scarborough introduced numbers of visitors to the simple pleasures of seaside life. In 1697 Celia Fiennes noted:

> On this Sand by the Seashore is ye Spaw well wch people frequent, and all the diversion is ye walking on the sand twice a day at ye Ebb of the tide and till its high tide and then they drink . . . It seems a pretty turbulent sea, I was on it in a little boate but found it very rough even just in ye harbour.

For some, the sea itself offered a diversion, as a visitor noted in 1732:

> It is the custom here not only for gentlemen but the ladies also, to bathe in the open sea. The gentlemen go out a little way in boats called cobbles, and jump in direct from them. The ladies have the conveniency of dressing gowns and guides, and there are little houses on the shore for them to retire and dress in.

By the early eighteenth century it was claimed that 'most of the Gentry of the North of England and Scotland resort hither in the season of the year', and while Scarborough clearly lacked the sparkle of the more illustrious southern spas, it could boast a variety of recreations – horse-racing on the sands, gaming rooms, theatre, dancing and a circulating library. By 1785 it was said that the town was 'long distinguished as one of the most ancient and respectable sea-bathing places in Great Britain'.

On the beach there was a line of twenty-six bathing machines from which 'two women attend each lady who bathes, as guides; and one man every gentleman who requires it.' And it was noticeable that it was the beach and the sea, as much as the spa, which increasingly became the focus of daily routines at Scarborough. By the turn of the century a local historian asserted that Scarborough perfectly fitted the rules for bathing established by Dr Russell. Rituals evolved for seabathing at Scarborough and elsewhere, generally guided by medical opinion.

> For those who are robust, the morning, before breakfast, is the best time; for those who are delicate, it may be better to take breakfast first, and bathe nearer noon. – Both should

plunge into the waves, and return immediately, – unless for particular reasons some delay is directed. The Guides, I know, have great faith in the number *three*, and often powerfully recommend three immersions. They who bathe for pleasure may without risk submit; but the delicate should return immediately, and be wiped dry, and in many cases put on a flannel gown for a moment, until the feet and legs are well-dried. In some cases cordials and previous exercise are necessary to ensure the glow, and may require friction with dry flannels all over.

By force of social habit, encouraged by medical and published advice, this pattern of seabathing had, by the late eighteenth century, become commonplace. Mornings were reserved for bathing, and in the process the focus of activity switched to life on the beach.

In the mornings Scarborough beach was usually crowded with strollers, bathers and riders. Visitors, nicknamed 'spaws' by the locals, found the beach a perfect playground for their children. 'To observe the little animals,' wrote a visitor in 1803, 'in the greatest degree of health and spirits, fabricating their pies and their castles in the sand, is a treat for a philosopher.' This Birmingham man, in Scarborough for his daughter's health, saw to it, throughout eleven weeks, that the girl rode daily, bathed every second day and drank water three times each day. Scarborough in the early years of the nineteenth century was a seaside town in a recognizably modern vein. But it was remote from any great centre of population, and travel was laborious and expensive. In an age when extended leisure was the preserve of the few, Scarborough as a resort was reserved for the 'better sorts', with the obvious exception of local · working people. And this pattern was repeating itself in the south.

Scarborough had become a regional seabathing resort largely by accident and while it could hope to attract visitors from the north and perhaps the Midlands, it was unlikely to appeal to London society. In the pre-railway age of difficult travel, the upper classes of the metropolis inevitably turned to closer seaside towns for their new-found pleasures and cures, drifting inexorably to the new resorts which began to emerge along the south coast and on the Thames estuary. Of all the southern resorts which developed by the end of the eighteenth century to cater for the ills and pleasures of fashionable society – Weymouth, Hastings, Folkestone, Southend, Margate, Ramsgate, Bognor, Lyme Regis and Brighton – the last was undoubtedly pre-eminent. As early as 1736 the Rev. William Clarke wrote:

> We are now sunning ourselves on the beach at Brighthelmstone . . . Such a tract of sea; such regions of corn . . . My morning business is bathing in the sea, and then buying fish; the evening is riding out for air, viewing the remains of old Saxon camps and counting the ships in the roads and the boats that are trawling.

Both the tide and the shingle made bathing at Brighton uncomfortable, but it was social pressure rather than the town's geography which helped to establish Brighton as a classic late-eighteenth-century seaside resort, for, like Bath earlier in the century, Brighton's reputation was launched by royal patronage.

In the September of 1783 the Prince of Wales paid his first visit to Brighton, returning in the following year, according to Christopher Hibbert, 'apparently on the advice of his physicians who had advocated sea-bathing as a cure for the swollen glands in his throat, an unsightly affliction which distressed him deeply'. The Prince's presence accelerated the upper-class drift to the town and was to be largely responsible for its characteristic tone of dissolute and abandoned enjoyment, which contrasted so sharply with the alleged medicinal attractions of the seaside. Perhaps the one cured the other. But the new social tone repelled some of the older visitors. According to the *Morning Post*:

> The visit of a certain gay, illustrious character at Brighton, has frightened away a number of old maids, who used constantly to frequent that place. This history of [his] gallantries . . . has something in it so voluminous, and tremendous to boot, that the old tabbies shake in their boots when his R— H— is mentioned.

The Prince's liaison with Mrs Fitzherbert provided the perfect excuse for setting up house in Brighton, drawing behind him a veritable army of acolytes, admirers and those merely anxious to follow the social patterns of royalty. When, after

1789, *émigré* Frenchmen fled from the Revolution, many found at Brighton, not simply a convenient landing-stage from the Dieppe packet but a colourful social life reminiscent of the recéntly toppled regime. With its flourishing air, its races, masques, balls and splendid buildings, Brighton took on an unmistakable upper-class tone (with the unhappy side effect that the town was even more expensive than London).

Just as the Prince's entourage rapidly changed Brighton's social style, so too did his architects, Henry Holland and John Nash, transform the town's physical face. Few could afford to emulate the lavish style of the Pavilion, but the royal example stimulated a wave of building which came to exemplify the best of seaside Regency architecture. In the words of Clifford Musgrave: 'The combined features of curved bays, long windows and iron railings became charmingly characteristic not only of hundreds of houses that were built [in Brighton] but in those of many other seaside resorts such as Hastings, Ramsgate, Margate, Weymouth, and eventually towns all over the British Isles.' Long after the noise and bustle of the Prince's Brighton had subsided, the architecture – like that of Bath – was to remain as a monument to a past phase of upper-class recreation.

Other seaside towns did more than copy the splendours of Brighton's architecture, for they, like Brighton itself, were deeply influenced by the legacy of the inland spas. Indeed, it is striking the degree to which the new seaside resorts adopted the physical and social styles and functions of the older spas – a clear indication of how the idea of 'taking the waters' was transplanted from spa to seaside. It was noticeable how the resorts became seaside replicas of the spas, offering those recreations to be found in the inland resorts. Assembly rooms, billiard and card rooms, tea rooms, theatres and libraries sprang up in most seaside resorts worthy of the name. The social tone of the resorts of the late eighteenth and early nineteenth centuries can be gauged by the facilities provided – and by the buildings they were housed in, just as, a century later, the more plebeian recreations of newer resorts were to indicate their new working-class clientele.

The fashionable rush to the sea was on well before the turn of the century and was captured by Cowper in his poem *Retirement*.

Your prudent grandmammas, ye modern belles,
Content with Bristol, Bath, and Tunbridge Wells,
When health required it, would consent to roam,
Else more attached to pleasures found at home,
But now alike, gay widow, virgin, wife,
Ingenious to diversify still life,
In coaches, chaises, caravans and hoys,
Fly to the coast for daily, nightly joys,
And all, impatient of dry land, agree,
With one consent to rush into the sea.

Yet the new resorts differed greatly one from another and the social nuances were swiftly reflected in contemporary prints. Brighton became fashionable, but Margate was rather low, being full of 'cits'. And even Brighton offended the more sedate. In 1788 John Byng found it 'in a fashionable unhappy bustle, with such a harpy set of painted harlots as appear to me as bad as Bond Street in the spring at three o'clock p.m. . . . Elegant and modest people will not abide the place.' Cowper, on the other hand, deplored Margate, writing to a friend in 1779:

But you think Margate more lively. So is a Cheshire cheese full of mites more lively than a sound one . . . I remember, too, that Margate, though full of company, was generally filled with such company, as people who were nice in the choice of their company, were rather fearful of keeping company with. The hoy went to London every week, loaded with mackerel and herrings, and returned, loaded with company. The cheapness of the conveyance made it equally commodious for dead fish and lively company.

It was no accident that Jane Austen's last book, *Persuasion*, published in 1818, was concerned with that society which found much of its social life beside the sea, at Lyme.

Anne and Henrietta, finding themselves the earliest of the party the next morning, agreed to stroll to the sea before breakfast. – They went to the sands, to watch the flowing of the tide, which a fine south-easterly breeze was bringing in with all the grandeur which so flat a shore admitted. They praised the morning; gloried in the sea; sympathised in the delight of the fresh-feeling breeze – and were silent; till Henrietta suddenly began again, with,

'Oh! yes – I am quite convinced that, with very few exceptions, the sea-air always does good. There can be no doubt of its having been the greatest service to Dr Shirley, after his illness, last spring twelvemonth. He declares himself, that coming to Lyme for a month, did him more good than all the medicine he took; and, that being by the sea, always made him feel young again.

Whatever diversions available at the resorts, mornings were reserved for bathing and, both to preserve modesty and to facilitate immersion in the sea, bathing machines were devised – the first apparently in Scarborough in the 1730s. Yet there were limits to contemporary modesty, for while some women bathed in cumbersome flannels, nude bathing was equally common. Not surprisingly, bathing, from an early date, aroused mixed passions; disapproval from the morally brittle, voyeurism from knots of men, and coyness bordering on panic on the part of some bathers. Throughout the history of seabathing, many people have bathed in the nude, largely because suitable bathing attire is a fairly recent invention, with the result that bathing has frequently produced squeals of moral outrage. In 1807, for example, Brighton Parish Vestry met to prevent 'the indecent practice of indiscriminate bathing in front of the town'. Two years later John Crunden, a local tailor, was fined for 'having daily exposed himself on the beach'. Such penalties had little effect however and naked men, reluctant to plunge into cold water, left themselves exposed to the public gaze too long for the liking of some contemporaries.

The custom rapidly spread to all social classes and in 1795 John Aiken, describing life in Liverpool, noted:

It is the custom with the lower class of people, of both sexes, for many miles up the country, to make an annual visit to Liverpool, for the purpose of washing away (as they seem to suppose) all the collected stains and impurities of the year. Being unable to afford a long stay, or to make use of artificial conveniences, they employ two or three days in strolling along shore, and dabbling in the salt-water for hours at each tide, covering the beach with their promiscuous numbers, and not much embarrassing themselves about appearances. As the practice, however, seems conducive both to health and pleasure, it is not to be wished that rigid notions of delicacy should interfere with this only mode which the poor have of enjoying it.

It troubled and concerned others however. Writing of Brighton in 1841, Dr A. B. Granville, the historian of the resorts, remarked:

> Many lacking the courage after they have stripped to the skin, will stand on the outer steps of the machine, shivering and hesitating, their persons in the meanwhile wholly exposed . . . No attempt has yet been made by the authorities to set this right, and the practice remains as a stain on the gentility of the Brighthelmstonians.

To encourage the more timorous to take the plunge, the seaside resorts had on hand a number of bathing women. These large, hardy females operated from the bathing machines, hovering in and on the edge of the water ready to plunge their customers under the waves. They were tough women, ready to withstand the rigours of hours in the water and able to thrust unwilling bathers below the surface for the necessary number of immersions. Perhaps the most celebrated was Brighton's Martha Gunn, a prominent figure on the Brighton beach for decades. One day in August 1807 the beach

> was thronged with ladies all anxious to make interest for a dip. The machines were in great request, though none could be run into the ocean in consequence of the heavy swell, but remained stationary at the water's edge, from which Martha Gunn and her robust female assistants took their charges, in their parti-coloured dresses, and gently held them to the breakers, which not so gently passed over them.

Royal patronage inevitably enhanced a dipper's reputation. Mrs Gunn was the Prince Regent's favourite, though he also suffered some robust treatment at the hands of her male contemporary, 'Old Smoker'. One day in 1787 the Prince set out to bathe despite the particularly rough sea.

'I shall bathe this morning, "Smoker".'
'No, no, Your Royal Highness, it's too dangerous.'
'But I will.'
'Come, come, this won't do . . . I'll be damned if you shall bathe. What do you think your royal father would think of me if you were drowned?'
'He would say, "This is all owing to you, 'Smoker'. If you had taken proper care of him, poor George would still be alive."'

Fortunately for 'Smoker', the Prince desisted.

A dipper at Southend, Mrs Myall, boasted of having 'been favoured with the attendance of her Royal Highness Princess Charlotte of Wales, and some of the first families, whose approbation she has received for her particular skill and tenderness'. No seaside resort wanting to offer bathing facilities could, by the turn of the century, afford to be without its bathing machines and attendant dippers, and the custom was to survive well into the nineteenth century. But the growth of more informal bathing, particularly after the arrival of train-borne hordes from the big cities, was to make the dippers redundant.

Brighton's rapid rise to pre-eminence was reflected in its population. Standing at about 2000 in 1760, by 1801 it was more than 7000 and by 1811 had risen to 12,000. But the increase in the next decade – to more than 24,000 – was even more startling (though these figures have to be set in the context of the country's overall population explosion). To cope with this expansion of permanent and transient population, buildings mushroomed (doubling in the years 1820–30); and all this in the reign of George IV who, as Prince of Wales, had done so much to establish the town's fortunes. The King had almost come to be synonymous with Brighton, having witnessed the blossoming of a distinguished town – with parades, crescents and squares – from a nondescript fishing village. When we remember the urban development in other parts of the country, where towns and cities tumbled in an unplanned chaos into the countryside, Brighton seems a triumph for order and good taste. Its elegance was that of a spa town, a fact reinforced in 1825 by the establishment of the 'German Spa' which helped partially to shift fashionable focus back to the pump-room and to enhance the town's reputation as a centre for medical cures. Yet it was ironic that this reversion to a more traditional form of taking the waters (in the case of the German Spa, artificial waters) should take place in the town which, more than any other, had brought polite interest to the seaside.

But the sea maintained its appeal, particularly after the opening, in 1823, of the Chain Pier, which facilitated regular sailings to Dieppe. The Pier also received the King's patronage, but its main custom was provided by the sick 'rendering it an open air hospital, and tempting one to impose upon the town the ancient Saxon designation of Bath – the sick man's city.' However, that most valuable of all Brighton's assets – royal patronage and residence – was soon to end, for the era of the railways, arriving in Brighton in 1841, brought uncouth hordes pressing their faces close to the royal persons who promptly took themselves off to the more secluded delights of the Isle of Wight.

Royal visits proved similarly influential at other resorts on the south coast. Whereas proximity to London was perhaps the most important feature of any would-be resort, the example of Weymouth – a long and troublesome drive from the capital – suggests the degree to which royal patronage could shape a town's fortunes. There were of course sound reasons why George III, following medical advice after his mental troubles of 1787–8, should seek fresh air far away from Brighton where his recalcitrant son had set up home. So in 1789 the royal party (happily, for the historian, with Fanny Burney in tow) descended on Weymouth. The journey became a triumphant procession, culminating in daily protestations of loyalty in Weymouth itself. The King slowly acclimatized himself to the sea air with plenty of exercise, sampling the local entertainments and taking medically supervised salt-water baths in his rooms. But all this was mere rehearsal for the sea itself and accordingly, on Sunday 7 July 1789 – watched by great crowds – George III took the royal plunge. 'Think but of the surprise of His Majesty when, the first time of his bathing, he had no sooner popped his royal head under water than a band of music concealed in a neighbouring machine, struck up "God save great George our King".'

The King clearly enjoyed Weymouth and although he returned regularly and enhanced the town's reputation, the tone of

Weymouth never approached the air of royal abandon which his son actively fostered along the coast at Brighton. Weymouth was, in fact, a better bathing spot, as Dr Granville pointed out:

> The sea-bathing is perfect at Weymouth . . . The sands over which the bathers have to walk are well-known, as being of the finest description, equal to those of Scarborough in the east, and Blackpool in the west, and superior to any other in the south. The declivity of the shore is almost imperceptible, and totally free from those obstructions which are noticed on many parts of the southern coast; so that the most timid lady may indulge in the great luxury of open sea-bathing, with the additional comfort of perfect security, and of sea-water pure, clean and transparent; in fact, genuine, unpolluted sea-water.

Weymouth was, however, too distant from London to become a major pre-industrial watering place, for those southern resorts which emerged by the late years of the eighteenth century were generally within a more manageable distance of the capital.

The most accessible towns from London were those which could be easily reached by boat down the Thames. By the early nineteenth century both Margate and Southend, for example, had become established resorts for London society. Seabathing at Margate had been well-established by mid eighteenth century and in 1753 a local Quaker, Benjamin Beale, added a refinement to local bathing machines in the form of an awning which covered the bather until totally immersed in the sea. Margate's natural advantages, 'the fineness of the beach – the purity of the air', ensured its swift rise as a resort, greatly assisted by the ease of travel from London by the 'hoys' or small sailing ships. In 1815 the first steam packets began to ply down the Thames, carrying 23,500 passengers in the first year. By 1830 – before the railways had begun to whisk even larger numbers of passengers around the country – the steamships carried 95,000 people between London and Margate. In 1831, some 2000 people arrived daily – after a journey of six and a half hours – and it was claimed that 'the trade of the town is almost entirely connected with the resort of visitors'.

Perhaps because of the ease of communication Margate,

despite its assembly rooms and its pretensions to ape its competitors on the south coast, was less exclusive: 'so common', in the words of a cartoon of 1820. Cheap transport, by ship, helped to democratize Margate as a resort, pointing the way to the developments of the railway age. It was clear, even before the coming of the railways, that English resorts, like English recreations in general, were differentiated by class. Class was already dividing Englishmen at play as surely as it divided them at work.

Southend was also approached from London by water and, once again, a royal visit helped to promote the town's fortunes. There, as at other resorts, a spate of building took place to cope with the growing number of visitors. Moreover, the nature and style of the buildings leave no doubt that the purpose was to re-create the image of the spa tradition and provide for visitors of a better class. A new hotel, a terrace, theatre and warm-water baths sprang up to cater for the routines of society by the sea. Once established as a fashionable resort, Southend began to draw upon the gentry of the Essex hinterland and, in addition to becoming a seaside retreat for Londoners, soon established itself as the centre of social life for a widely scattered and relatively inaccessible rural community.

Though easily approached by sea, Southend's beach made landing rather difficult. A half-mile wooden jetty was isolated at low tide and consequently a quarter-mile of shingle known as the 'Hard' was laid out to sea.

> There follows a space of clear water, even at low tide, which divides the termination of the Hard and a cluster of piles called the *mount* . . . To this mount when it is low water, the Gravesend and Southend steamers land their passengers in the summer, who are then boated over to the Hard, and hence walk to the jetty. A[t] high tide, and when the weather is not boisterous, the steamers land their passengers at the jetty itself.

An older pier had catered for the old sailing ships, but the inauguration of a steamship service in 1819 required a longer pier. New piers were pushed further and further out to sea, eventually culminating in the famous pier stretching one and a quarter miles. Southend was, because of its peculiar geography, among the early pioneers in pier-making, heralding that aspect of seaside architecture which was to characterize English resorts through to the present day.

In the north, Scarborough's unique attractions had for a long time drawn the local leisured classes. But in the last two decades of the eighteenth century other northern seaside villages began to witness changes of fortune. Parts of the Lancastrian coast, for instance, were sufficiently close to the expanding inland urban areas to encourage the emergent local middle class to emulate their southern peers by taking their families to the seaside – despite the unmade roads. Significantly, property owners in the small village of Blackpool began to place advertisements in Manchester newspapers in 1785. In June of that year a Blackpool proprietor informed the 'Gentry and Public'

> that he has completely furnished and fitted up a commodious genteel house in an eligible situation and that he hopes by his accommodation to merit the encouragement of such ladies and gentlemen as may be pleased to favour him with their company. NB. A bathing machine will be kept for the use of his friends.

The appeal was clearly directed to the better-off in the Manchester district, but even more significant was the forging of links between what was to become the capital of the textile region and the resort which, in years to come, was to exemplify holidays for northern textile operatives. Two years later, with a view to reinforcing the genteel appeal of Blackpool proprietors, further advertisements appeared in the Manchester newspapers. John Bonney's hotel had a tariff which distinguished by class; 'Ladies and gentlemen, 2s. 2d. per each day; children 1s 6d.; servants, 1s. 6d.' In the same vein, in July,

> Mr Sharples, Blackpool, begs to inform the public that he has fitted up his home in a very genteel manner for the reception of ladies and gentlemen who resort to Blackpool during the bathing season. The house is very pleasantly situated and contains 18 lodging rooms; a coach house, stabling for 16 horses and other conveniences. The terms are: For ladies and gentlemen, 2s a day, Children and servants 1s. 6d.

By the early 1790s that entrepreneurial mentality which came to personify generations of flinty Blackpool landladies was well in evidence: George Cook, a local hotelier, who perhaps utilized his experiences of life in America, began to provide a wide range of facilities and commodities for potential clients. And, again, he appealed to them in the Manchester newspapers:

> Gunpowder, Hyson, Souchong and Congou teas of the first quality; White's Cocoa, coffee, chocolate, loaf and brown sugar, sago, tapioca, spices of all kinds and other groceries; Jewellry of the newest fashion from one of the first houses in London. An assortment of hosiery, millinery, linen, drapery . . . bathing caps and dresses . . . The public room will be furnished with a library of books, a large collection of copper plate engravings . . . newspapers and magazines etc.; and in the billiard room is a handsome table and everything necessary to render that genteel amusement agreeable to the company. Ladies may have anything made in the genteelest manner and at the shortest notice.

By the turn of the century people of quality could travel to Blackpool knowing that the town could provide, on a limited scale, a pale imitation of social life at home or a trip to the socially superior resorts of the south. Anxious to promote its nearest resort, the *Blackburn Mail* of 24 June 1795 trumpeted its belief that 'we may justly call Blackpool the first watering place in the kingdom, whether we consider the salubrity of the air, the beauty of the scenery, the excellence of the accommodation, or the agreeable company of which it is the general resort.' In fact similar claims were made for any resort anxious to capitalize on the growth in seaside visits.

Northerners may have found Blackpool overwhelmingly genteel – an image actively promoted by the residents – but outsiders were generally unimpressed by the social graces of the town's visitors. Catherine Hutton of Birmingham wrote home in 1788 describing the other visitors to Blackpool:

> These people are, in general, of a species called Boltoners, that is, rich, rough honest manufacturers of the town of Bolton, whose coarseness of manners is proverbial even among their countrymen. The other houses [hotels] are

frequented by better company, that is Lancashire gentry, Liverpool Merchants, and Manchester manufacturers. I find here that I have no equals but the lawyers, for those who are my equals in fortune are distinguished by their vulgarity, and those who are my equals in manners, are above me in station.

Catherine Hutton's character sketches were shrewd and telling: 'The Boltoners are sincere, good humoured and noisy. The Manchestrians reserved and purse-proud; the Liverpoolians free and open as the ocean on which they get their riches.' And it was this image of plain-speaking – if rather loud – industrial middle men which struck Dr Granville when he visited Blackpool fifty years later.

With the massive growth of population in near-by textile towns by the early nineteenth century, the Lancashire coastal towns provided an accessible outlet from the grime and almost unremitting toil of industrial life. As a result, Blackpool, Lytham, and Southport began to receive armies of day-trippers long before the railway companies forged their iron links between the industrial towns and the coast. In 1813 the traveller Richard Ayton found in Blackpool

> crowds of poor people from the manufacturing towns, who have a high opinion of the efficacy of bathing, maintaining that in the months of August and September there is physic in the sea – physic of a most comprehensive description, combining all the virtues of all the drugs in the doctor's shop, and of course a cure for all varieties of disease.

To reach the sea's cures, the poor travelled to Blackpool on foot and, once there, subjected themselves to the harsh and unpleasant regime of salt-water bathing and drinking which had become fashionable among their superiors.

> The earliest act of the morning is a draught of salt water, a quart, and sometimes two, which is followed, under the notion of fortifying the stomach by an equal quantity of gin and beer. This mixture swallowed, a man is properly prepared for the bath, in which he continues to paddle either in or out of his clothes for the remainder of the day.

At peak summer time, Blackpool beach was 'darkened with

thick clusters of people, full of motion, and continually splashing in and out of the water'.

Ayton found similar scenes to the north at Poulton-le-Sands (later Morecambe) where cartloads of visitors swelled the small village to bursting point. Again, the visitors were often working people from near-by industrial towns, who had 'come for the benefit of the physic in the sea'. Heavy drinking and eating in the evenings required sharp treatment the following morning, and by 7 a.m. the seaside revellers were alert and lively again, 'with appetites sharpened by bathing, and copious draughts of salt-water'.

But for all relatively poor industrial workers the prime virtue of any particular seaside spot was its accessibility to their home town. While more prosperous inhabitants of the industrial towns had the necessary time and money to reach remoter spots on the Lancashire coast (or even to travel south and east) industrial workers could visit the sea only when it was close, and easily and cheaply reached. Moreover, in the absence of regulated and guaranteed holidays, the opportunities for travel to the seaside were extremely restricted.

Working people in Preston were ideally placed to visit Blackpool, with the result that many of the middle-class visitors from Manchester who had once been drawn there began to look elsewhere. Southport offered an ideal, quiet alternative, for it was more difficult to reach and consequently less dominated by poorer visitors. By 1841 Dr Granville noted that it was to Southport that

> the Manchester factor and artisan – the rich and the 'middling comfortable' – repair during two months of the year, either for a week or two's residence, or for a mere frolic. At that period, one may see the walls of that smoky city placarded with 'Cheap travelling to Southport' – 'Only five hours to Southport' – 'Excursions to Southport'.

Southport began to develop later than Blackpool. In 1806 it was claimed to have been 'scarcely hitherto known' but within twenty years it was attracting the 'busy burghers' of Manchester. Bathing flourished: 'At the height of the tide every machine is in motion, carrying indiscriminately, occupants of either sex, at no unsociable distance from each other.' The gentility which was

Southport's early virtue was reinforced by the encouragement of large-scale land-holdings which guaranteed that the growing town would not be developed on a piecemeal, small-plot basis, but rather offered scope for the development of more substantial properties. Whereas Blackpool was rapidly chopped into sub-divided plots, Southport's urban growth was planned and orderly, and the resulting differences were to a large extent to account for the different social appeal of the two towns.

Lytham, a few miles south of Blackpool, was similar to Southport in its peacefulness. In 1813 its virtues were noted by one visitor, who thought that 'the numerous tribes of gamblers, unhappy profligators and fashionable swindlers find rapine and employment elsewhere'. The devout Jonathan Peel, calico printer of Accrington, holidayed at Lytham 'and each Sunday one of the two bathing machines the place was endowed with carried him and one or two elderly friends to the small white-walled church in the fields'. But by the 1820s Lytham's peace was shattered by the overspill of visitors from Blackpool to the north. In August 1824 the *Preston Chronicle* noted that both Blackpool and Lytham had 'never witnessed such crowds of visitors of various classes as have this week continued to flock to them in search of health, pleasure and relaxation'. By 1828 Lytham was completely overwhelmed by August seabathers from Preston. The sheer pressure of population had transformed a sleepy village into a congested, popular resort for transient working people from the nearest industrial city – a pattern which was to recur time and again from the 1840s onwards, when the railways nosed their way to the coastline.

As early as the 1820s it was apparent that there was enormous potential for transporting thousands of people out of the cities to the coast or country. But pre-railway travel facilities were inadequate to the demand already manifested on those few summer days when industrial workers found themselves free from work. From the very early days of the resorts it was clear that their development revolved to a large extent around that of transport. This was to remain a constant feature. In the first years of the nineteenth century it was obvious that seaside resorts had tremendous appeal. The difficulty was how to get there.

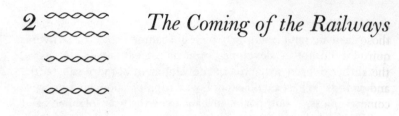
∽∽∽∽∽ When William Hutton took his family from Birmingham to Blackpool in 1788, they endured a journey of three days. Even the much shorter journey from Manchester via Preston lasted from early morning until late evening. By the 1830s, however, the journey between Preston and Blackpool had become easier thanks to a paved road. Visitors to Brighton in the late eighteenth century were lucky, for they travelled over what was considered to be the best road in Britain and the London–Brighton route undoubtedly benefited (as did others) from the introduction of Royal Mail coaches after 1784. The new lightweight coaches carried mail and passengers further and faster than ever before, largely through the use of relays of horses at ten-mile intervals. In 1801 the more leisurely coaches from London took twelve hours to reach Brighton, but by 1810 a new night Royal Mail coach had cut the time to eight hours. By 1823, forty-eight coaches plied daily between the capital and Brighton and road improvements steadily reduced the travelling time. In 1830 it could be covered in four and a half hours. But Brighton was exceptional both in the volume of traffic it attracted and in the social class of passengers.

The cost of coach travel was high. When a new service was opened between Halifax and Blackpool in 1782, it cost 18s. 6d.; two years later a new line from Manchester to Blackpool cost 14s. The cost of journeys throughout the country varied between 2½d. and 3d. per mile, though the less prosperous could reduce the cost by travelling outside the coach, or by taking the more ponderous stage wagons for 1d. per mile. But in all cases, coach travel was clearly beyond the reach of most poorer passengers.

The main problem facing coach travel was the condition of the roads, but pressure for road improvements began to come from those whose growing industrial and commercial activity required a more effective means of communication. Furthermore, the sheer growth in population meant a massive rise in people and goods travelling along inadequate roads. But it was commercial pressure which helped to generate the late-eighteenth-century upsurge in turnpike trusts which, quite literally, paved the way between the centres of population and made possible the smoother transportation of people, raw materials and goods. By the 1830s, despite piecemeal development, the turnpike trusts (which utilized the innovations and expertise of the new engineers led by Telford, Metcalfe and MacAdam) had created a national network of roads. Times of journeys fell dramatically and the volume of road travel increased accordingly. It has been calculated that by the mid 1830s fifteen times as many people were travelling in coaches compared with the 1790s. Moreover, it was now easier on most routes (perhaps for the first time in English history) to travel by coach rather than horseback.

The poor, however, still walked or, if lucky, hitched lifts on carts. Richard Ayton noted of Blackpool visitors in 1813, 'Most of them come hither in carts, but some will walk in a single day from Manchester, distant more than forty miles.' For such people, distance to the coast was of paramount importance and was to remain so until a relatively cheap form of transport was devised. When, in the 1830s and 1840s, a new railway system rapidly sprang up around the country, it produced a profound social revolution which is difficult to overstress.

Dr Granville, whose travel to the resorts was greatly eased by the new railway lines, was dazzled, like so many of his contemporaries, by the potential of the railways – for good and ill. It is, he said, 'unquestionable, that to afford cheap and speedy means of travelling for the people, is to induce people to travel who would otherwise have staid at home; and if this process is to go on much further, the whole nation, at length, will be on the move'. One consequence was that many thousands – like Granville himself – found themselves travelling by train to the seaside.

The economic and technological origins of the railway age were complex, but the result was a swift proliferation of lines

across the face of the country. The railways seemed to offer un-
limited economic rewards and, as a result, railway companies
mushroomed, capital for investment was plentiful and Parliament was eager to push through special Acts needed to sanction
railway development. There were, inevitably, booms and slumps,
for although the mania for railways encouraged wise and viable
ventures, it also produced the risky and foolhardy, particularly
in the years 1844–7. But amid the fortunes made and lost, and
ill-conceived lines which failed to leave the planning stage, the
achievements of the railway age were staggering and rapidly
helped to transform an embryonic industrial nation into a
modern economy, able to marshal its materials and goods by
means of a relatively efficient system of communications.

Few aspects of English life escaped the direct impact – or
distant shadow – of the railways. And among the 7500 miles
of track in existence by mid century, a number reached out to
the coasts. By the mid 1840s those popular seaside towns on the
Lancashire and Yorkshire coasts which had limited access to the
industrial interior, were either connected directly by rail or
were within striking distance of a railway station. Similarly,
on the south coast. Brighton was linked to London, thus making
even the improved coach services of earlier years seem relatively
crude and slow.

Much of the financial impetus behind the establishment of
railway lines was the belief that goods traffic would increase
substantially. But in the event, the upsurge in passenger traffic
was even more staggering. When, in June 1838, Newcastle was
linked to Carlisle the number of people travelling between the
two towns increased elevenfold, many being attracted by the
special excursions laid on for poorer travellers at holiday periods.
For workers in Dundee the seaside resort of the Ferry had
previously been approached by foot or cart, but in 1839, in
seven months alone, no fewer than 61,876 third-class tickets
were issued for the new railway journey between the two points.

In fact the railway companies of the 1830s (not unlike the
airline companies of the 1950s) were originally unaware of the
economic potential of a mass, low-income passenger market and
they concentrated instead on more prosperous travellers. It is
characteristic and significant that when the directors of railway
companies put their minds to the task of providing more com-

prehensive passenger facilities, they ordered their rolling stock, prices and passengers by *class*. The railways exemplified the degree to which the language of class permeated English society. At work, at home, at rest and even at play and travelling, Englishmen were assigned to a preordained place; on the railways, from the late 1830s, the English working man took his cheap, but primitively crude, third-class seat. Cramped, open to the elements, unsprung and frequently dangerous, the third-class coaches nevertheless made it possible for low-income groups to take to the trains, especially after Gladstone's Railway Act of 1844, which obliged railway companies to make provision for the 'labouring classes'.

Travel cost could be lowered still further by provision of special excursion trains, and from an early date the companies realized the economic virtue of organizing such excursions. Thomas Cook, though not the first to organize excursion trains, was primarily responsible for establishing the commercial benefits of special trains when, in 1841, he arranged a trip from Leicester to Loughborough for 570 temperance supporters. Encouraged by this early success, Cook branched out, organizing trips to other Midland towns and beauty spots, to Scarborough, Manchester, Liverpool and, of course, to the 1851 Exhibition (when some 165,000 people travelled with his organization). Arranging for travel by night wherever possible (so as to avoid cutting into the working day, yet providing travellers with ample daylight time for enjoyment), Cook reduced the cost of travel and firmly established the attraction of excursion trains – for passengers and companies alike.

The Lancashire textile towns offered scope for similar enterprise, particularly after 1840 when the new line from Preston reached the developing port of Fleetwood. Within a month the trains were ferrying unprecedented thousands to Fleetwood, from where they travelled the few miles south to Blackpool. According to a Bolton newspaper: 'The town literally swarms with human beings, and every day fresh loads roll in covered with dust and crying out for beds . . . The Fleetwood and Wyre railroad seems to have contributed largely to this extraordinary influx of visitors.' In 1842 an excursion train of twenty-seven coaches carried 2364 Sunday-school teachers and pupils from Preston to Fleetwood. 'The whole multitude were engaged in singing hymns.' In August 1844 the *Preston Chronicle* proclaimed, 'Cheap trains and pleasure excursions are now all the go and fashion.' A week earlier, thirty-eight carriages (all but nine of them third class) had gone from Preston to Fleetwood. 'One thousand seven hundred, men, women and children, chiefly of the working classes, on a Sunday excursion.'

Such trips became commonplace in the textile towns, as schools, churches and charitable manufacturers laid on excursions to the coast, though this is not to say that everyone could expect to enjoy such a visit. To celebrate the repeal of the Corn Laws in 1846, Richard Cobden gave his Chorley employees a day's wage and a trip to Fleetwood. Led by two bands, 1000 passengers, many carrying flags and banners, squeezed into thirty-nine coaches for a day by the sea. The extension of the line to Blackpool in that same year further encouraged excursion travel, as trains packed with textile operatives travelled to the coast on high days and the infrequent holidays. During Whit week 1848 it was estimated that 116,000 trippers left Manchester; by 1850 it had risen to 202,543. The sheer pressure of numbers began to reshape the social character of the resorts, more particularly of Blackpool which, at the height of the season, had become unmistakably plebeian – a town which respectable visitors frowned upon. 'Unless immediate steps are taken,' said the *Preston Pilot* in 1851, 'Blackpool as a resort for respectable visitors will be ruined ... Unless the cheap trains are discontinued or some effective regulation made for the management of the thousands who visit the place, Blackpool property will be depreciated past recovery.'

A similar story was repeated wherever a new branch or main line linked an industrial town to the coast. The impact of trippers on Brighton was, if anything, even more profound. In the 1830s that town's fortunes had suffered decline, but the direct link to London, opened in 1841, once again drew fashionable attention to Brighton. It also brought crowds of less prosperous visitors of whom the town had little experience and for whom it had even less liking, and Brighton, like Blackpool, began, on certain days, to take on a plebeian tone.

I took the train to Brighton – I walked beside the sea,
And thirty thousand Londoners were there along with me.

We crowded every lodging, and we lumbered each hotel,
Sniffed the briny for an appetite, and dined extremely well.

Brighton's population leaped from 46,000 in 1841 to 65,000
ten years later and the impact of the railways was similarly
registered in local house-building. In the decade before the
railway was opened, only 437 houses were built, but between
1841 and 1851 2806 were constructed. In these years Brighton
became 'the lungs of the capital' and in 1851 it was noted, 'The
number of passengers brought into the town daily by the railways is astonishing. On holiday occasions, in fine weather, there
seldom arrive fewer than 5000 visitors in the London trains.
The number of passengers in one week in May 1850 was up-
wards of 73,000.'

Not all excursions went to the sea of course. Indeed, the most
striking vindication of excursion travel was to the Great
Exhibition of 1851. Some 775,000 excursionists travelled to
London from the north of England alone, while the total
number of visitors who used the railways was estimated at
5 million. Thousands similarly travelled to the countryside or
even to neighbouring towns and cities. But it was the seaside
resorts which exemplified the enormous benefits of a railway
link. To secure a railway line to the nearest centre of population
became a consuming passion among those anxious to promote
a resort's development. When, for instance, Torquay was given
a rail link in 1848, a public holiday was declared. Many, however, resisted the approach of the railways, and opposition was
frequently couched in exclusive class terms. An opponent in
Scarborough, anxious to maintain the town's isolation, had 'no
wish for a greater influx of vagrants, and those who have no
money to spend'. It was inevitably a losing battle and in July
1845 the first train arrived from York, pulling thirty-five first-
class coaches. Within a month a new pattern was established,
when excursion trains arrived from Wakefield and Newcastle.
To cope with such waves of transient visitors, the resorts
were forced to expand. Indeed the rate of urban growth of
seaside towns was greater than that of any other kind of English
town. Taken together, the fifteen major watering places (in-
cluding four inland spas) showed a population increase between
1801 and 1851 of 254 per cent, a rate of increase which Professor

Gilbert has described as higher 'than that of London, or of fifty-one manufacturing towns, twenty-eight mining and hardware towns, twenty-six seaports and ninety-nine country towns'.

Provision of cheap excursion tickets was not easily achieved, however, for it involved a fundamental obstacle which had, since time out of mind, dogged the limited leisure pursuits of common people. For most working people, the sole day regularly free from work was Sunday, and to travel to the seaside (or play football – or take part in any organized leisure) was to affront the public sensibility of the powerful Victorian Sabbatarian lobby. Pre-industrial recreations had been restricted, frowned upon and even outlawed for similar reasons, particularly in the Puritan years of the sixteenth and seventeenth centuries. Complaints against Sunday travel and recreation were to echo through the Press, Parliament and the boardrooms of the railway companies as the godly sought to prevent further violations of the Sabbath by the train. The arguments are revealing and, in the process, the degree to which the years of Victorian England witnessed a secularization of social life can be gauged by the gradual transmutation of the holy day into the holiday.

From an early date, Sunday travel was anathema to many, not merely within the church. Travel to the coast, like most forms of popular leisure, was bitterly resisted at a time when many of the resisters, paradoxically, admitted the social and physical benefits of providing healthy leisure and recreation for poorer urban dwellers. The provision of leisure facilities for working people in the early Victorian city was virtually absent, as a contemporary noted in 1844: 'If the people of Manchester want to go out on a Sunday, where must they go? There are no public promenades, no avenues, no public gardens, and no public common . . . everything in the suburbs is closed against them; everything is private property.' By the mid 1840s many Englishmen (and foreign visitors too) were struck by the degree to which the joint forces of urbanization and industrialization had destroyed England's pre-industrial recreational patterns. Time and again, commentators in the 1830s and 1840s returned to the problem of leisure and recreation among working people. In 1833 Dr Kay wrote to a Select Committee:

At present the whole population of Manchester is without any season of recreation, and is ignorant of all amusements, excepting that very small portion which frequents the theatre. Healthful exercise in the open air is seldom or never taken by the artizans of this town . . . One reason of this state of the people is, that all scenes of interest are remote from the town.

That same Committee finally concluded that 'some Open Places reserved for the amusement (under due regulations to preserve order) of the humbler classes, would assist to wean them from low and debasing pleasures.'

But little was done in that decade or the next to alleviate the worst excesses of cramped urban life. In 1840 an observer noted of Manchester operatives that 'the whole Sunday is too frequently lost in either drinking or inactive idleness'. In Birmingham in 1842 it was claimed, 'The want of some place of recreation for the mechanic is an evil which presses very heavily upon these people, and to which many of their bad habits may be traced.' A Sheffield cutler, aged fifty in 1843, had seen the deterioration in local leisure facilities in his lifetime:

Thirty years ago it had numbers of places as common where youths and men could have taken exercise at cricket, quoits, football and other exercises . . . Scarce a foot of all these common wastes remain for the enjoyment of the industrial classes . . . To the want of proper places for healthful recreation may be attributed, in a measure, the great increase of crime in this town and neighbourhood.

And contemporaries repeated a similar tale from all of England's major towns, from Manchester, Birmingham, Sheffield, Wolverhampton, Liverpool, Leeds and Durham.

The arguments of the 1840s, which focused on the issue of Sunday trains, embraced both the need to re-establish regular breaks from work and the contradictory insistence on preserving the Sabbath untrammelled by leisure. Consequently the debate about Sabbatarianism frequently opened up a wider discourse about the need to shorten the working week, for if the Sabbath was to be kept holy, provision would clearly have to be made for rest and recreation on some other day. Lord John Manners,

M.P., wrote enthusiastically in favour of restoring 'NATIONAL HOLY DAYS and RECREATIONS' but constantly came against the industrialists' argument that 'time is money, and we cannot afford it'. But he argued, 'If games and sports are right on Sunday afternoons, then they ought to be restored: if they are wrong, and Sundays are to be kept as strictly religious festivals, then it must be right . . . to provide for their celebration on other days.'

Sunday trains, of any kind, but especially excursion trains, triggered off a pamphlet war in the 1840s as Sabbatarians sought to prove the theological, economic, moral and even divine objections to Sunday travel. One critic intoned that 'some gentlemen are apt to imagine that they befriend the working classes when they promote a little Sunday work for them, and Sunday recreation. But this is a great mistake . . . The railways and the tea-gardens cannot be kept but by the labour of multitudes deprived of their recreations themselves.' Until the 1850s the prime Sabbatarian battle was to prevent Sunday becoming part of the railways' week – an objection made virtually impossible by the growing complexity and size of the railway system that required constant control and movement. But excursionists posed a particularly severe threat to the peace of the Sabbath. George Hudson, the railway king, argued convincingly that a ban on Sunday travel would hit the poorest hardest of all, for the more prosperous had the means and opportunity to travel whenever they liked. *Punch* made much the same comment, in its own sarcastic way. For first-class passengers, morals 'are the same on all days of the week . . . being accustomed to amuse themselves all the six days of the week, it would be cruel to deprive them of recreation on the seventh.' But for third-class passengers 'to travel on Sunday is a heinous crime . . . Toil and hardship are their portion during the week, and enjoyment on the Sunday would make them discontented with their lot.' There was, however, an undoubtedly genuine fear among churchmen that, thanks to excursion trains, the tendency had grown 'to desert the church and to spend the Sunday as a holiday'.

Much of the drive behind Sabbatarianism was the desire to deny the nation any real alternative to church attendance. But the railways proved more and more seductive – sometimes to the alarm even of the railway companies. Following a visit of 1250 West Riding textile operatives to Hull, the board of the Hull railway company decided to ban 'excursions of mere pleasure leading inevitably to most extensive desecration of the Lord's Day'. This attitude persisted right through the nineteenth century; as late as 1895 the 'Anti-Sunday-Travelling Union' had 22,440 members. Such powerful opposition was able inevitably to restrain Sunday travel; tickets were issued for departure on Saturday – to return on Monday; by the mid 1860s, parts of forty lines were closed to Sunday traffic. And railway companies began to relax their opposition only at the turn of the century when road traffic began to compete for the mass Sunday market.

In the teeth of such opposition, seaside trippers would, in many areas, need to travel on weekdays. Unfortunately, few working people were free to take regular breaks in the week. Even Saturday was a working day and the evolution of Saturday – or part of it – free from work, brought about a movement whose aims were to liberate working people from the severe restraints of early industrial society. The idea that Saturday ought to be a holiday was slow in gaining acceptance, but by the mid 1860s, under pressure from the unions and influential opinion which stressed the social and physical benefits of guaranteed breaks from work, increasing numbers of people came to enjoy free Saturday afternoons. Lecturing to the Y.M.C.A. in the 1850s, James Millar, Professor of Surgery at Edinburgh, linked the need for a free Saturday to the campaign to preserve the Sabbath: 'Early closing is the key to the Sabbath. The Saturday afternoon is the time for recreation; that is the time for the steamboat trips and cheap railway trains, and for opening Crystal Palaces and British Museums.'

It was testimony to the attractions of the seaside that, despite the severe economic and social restraints on popular leisure and travel, the resorts grew more dramatically than other cities. In 1851 the census noted: 'Seaside resorts have expanded more rapidly than any other group of English towns and, in doing so, have overtaken inland spas.' Of the ten major seaside resorts, Brighton was by far the largest in population – more than four times larger than Hastings, its nearest rival.

Brighton	65,569	Torquay	7,903
Hastings	16,966	Scarborough	12,915
Ramsgate	11,838	Whitby	10,899
Margate	10,099	Southport	4,765
Weymouth	9,458	Blackpool	c. 2,000

Of these ten resorts, six were in the south and four in the north and, though Southport and Blackpool were by far the smallest, they nonetheless managed to cater for the popular demand from the conglomeration of textile towns. It is clear that the settled size of a resort bore only the vaguest relationship to the size of its transient population at the height of the season. It is also clear that the southern resorts, more so than their northern counterparts, were not merely places for the passing tripper, but also settled homes for many people who sought a healthier town or a peaceful spot for retirement.

The railways not only brought unprecedented numbers to the English coast but also stimulated further building, making possible the large-scale movement and perfection of new building materials.

The seaside resorts in the 1840s were characterized by their own dramatic growth. At Blackpool new large hotels sprang up on vacant land and on sites previously occupied by cottages. There, and at Brighton, these new hotels faced the sea; hoteliers and financiers sought to present their visitors with elegant and panoramic views of the sea and shoreline. As old fishing villages were gradually transformed from small knots of cottages into substantial towns, the physical focus of the towns changed. Whereas, before, buildings were generally crowded together, the new buildings were strung out along the coastline so that the sea-front became the centre of the town and the focus of the town's architecture and social life.

In 1851 a contemporary noted of Brighton that 'the greatly increased facilities of access afforded by the railway between Brighton and the metropolis has caused a considerable demand for house accommodation, to meet which, building is going on extensively'. Street maps show that within a decade of the railway's arrival in Brighton, where previously there had been vacant land, new houses were crowding close to the railway line. Blackpool was similarly transformed by the railways, but there the volume of building seems not to have kept pace with the increase in visitors. As a result Blackpool developed a notoriety for difficult and uncomfortable accommodation and long after the coming of the railways, even prosperous visitors had to take what was available and be content to have a roof over their heads.

In Blackpool, prices for accommodation rose alarmingly after the coming of the railway. In 1841 Dr Granville had been struck by the hotels 'in which the highest charge for board and excellent living is only five shillings a day, and in some cases, as low as three shillings'. But the railways put an end to that and it is clear that the post-railway inflation made overnight visits to Blackpool too expensive for low-income visitors. Yet it is also true that working-class visitors to Blackpool increased many times in the 1840s, the very great majority going as day-trippers. This meant the evolution of a new urban phenomenon – a town literally swamped by invading visitors who sought entertainment, refreshment and fun, but a town which was not expected to accommodate the bulk of its visitors overnight. Market towns had of course traditionally coped with similar short-lived migrations of people, but the scale and size of the visitors to the seaside made these seasonal migrations a qualitatively different social force. The pattern repeated itself in the 1850s as new railway lines connected resorts – Southport and Morecambe for example – to the industrial towns of Lancashire and Yorkshire. Each opening heralded fresh scenes of mass travel as thousands poured to the coast from the industrial towns. Clearly, the resorts could not cater instantly with such numbers, but the milling visitors provided great scope and challenge to the entrepreneurs who scurried there to fill the social and leisure void with their donkeys, music, games, acts and trinkets.

Seaside resorts faced a peculiar species of problem shared by all areas of urban growth in the nineteenth century – namely, how to control and regulate the physical and human development of towns. Residents of Blackpool, for instance, had to turn their attention to the complex and expensive question of health and cleanliness – but their slowness in controlling the attendant stench and filth, seems not to have repelled either fashionable or working-class visitors. In any case, it is unlikely to have been worse than many of the visitors' home towns.

Railways were now the key to the resorts' development. Railway lines designed for other purposes could have the side-effect of transforming a near-by coastal town. When in 1848 a railway line was opened between Chester and Holyhead (thus connecting London to Holyhead), the coastal town of Rhyl found itself on the railway map and, whereas in 1800 there were only two buildings in the town, after 1848 house- and hotel-building expanded. By 1852 a local guidebook listed 212 lodging-houses, and the railway companies began to offer the usual range of children's, seasonal and excursion tickets to the town. Inevitably Rhyl's proponents discovered health-giving qualities unknown before the railways came. 'Its position has seemed to me favourable to health and I have on more than one occasion sent patients there and especially for certain cardiac affections.'

The commercial potential of an embryonic seaside town often attracted the railway, and indeed the railway companies were often instrumental in financing, developing and owning substantial parts of the new resorts. George Hudson, always anxious to expand his considerable business empire, linked the fishing town of Whitby to his major railway network, speculating heavily in hotels and boarding-houses in the resort. Whitby's fortunes – unlike Hudson's – prospered, and were rooted in the railway links with the rest of Yorkshire. The transformation of Bournemouth by the railways was even more dramatic. The first house was built there in 1812 and in 1841 there were still fewer than thirty buildings. But the peripatetic Dr Granville – anxious to find the perfect seaside spa – gave the hamlet the seal of his considered approval: 'I look upon Bournemouth, and its yet unformed colony, as a perfect discovery among the sea-nooks one longs to have for a real invalid, and as the realisation of a *desideration* we vainly thought to have found elsewhere on the south coast of England.' Despite such praise, Bournemouth was a long way from London or the industrial cities, and its growth was slow and limited. But in the decade after the coming of the railways in 1870 the town's population almost tripled (from 5896 to 16,859). Before the railways came, the town was rather remote, and only travellers intending to stay there undertook the journey. Hence, in the years when many other resorts were developing to cater for day trippers, Bournemouth slipped snugly into the role of a slumbering resort for the prosperous sick and elderly.

Trains came late to the West Country, a fact bemoaned in the most obviously saucy way, by the *Western Times* in 1844: 'Increased intercourse with the most populous districts of England cannot but prove highly advantageous to the lovely spinster of Devon.' But once the railways began to appear in Devon, they both killed off the county's inland towns and markets and vitalized local seaside towns (which to a certain extent benefited from the country's rural depopulation). The railway reached Torquay in 1848, to be followed by bands of retired professional people, invalids and middle-class holiday-makers. Cheap-day excursionists, who so revolutionized resorts elsewhere, did not arrive until the last quarter of the century. In Devon as a whole, as in the country at large, the railways transformed the older watering places (of Sidmouth, Teign-mouth, Exmouth and Torquay) into holiday resorts. But the distance from the big cities guaranteed for the county a certain delayed immunity from the hordes which swamped other resorts, and it was to be the greater freedom – and extra cash – of the late century which enabled working people belatedly to look to Devon for day trips.

Morecambe, too, became a viable resort thanks to the arrival of the trains. The small village of Poulton, which until mid century attracted a trickle of summer visitors, became an object of interest for a railway company keen to find an outlet for local pig-iron and a port for the Irish ferries. With a new line opened in 1848 the potential resort was linked to the in-dustrial hinterland, but both local landowners and the com-mercially minded railway company were anxious to attract a better sort of tourist than working people, 'birds of passage whose residence does not extend over more than two or three days'. Once again, however, it was to be the greater financial freedoms brought about by the social and economic revolution of the last years of the century which enabled working people to turn to Morecambe – and other resorts – in significant numbers. Those resorts which felt the full force of working-class ex-cursionists in the early railway years were generally those with an established tradition as a popular resort. And there was a corollary to the general rule that seaside towns boomed after the arrival of the railway; where a town was by-passed, it often withered.

The railways were themselves a function of a new iron age in which men of enterprise and imagination were able to manipulate natural elements into highly efficient machines for the use of man. Mechanical and metallurgical developments were, at the same time, responsible for major changes in the shipping industry, where steamships began to make an impact. One historian of transportation has claimed that after 1830 'the increased scale of both passenger and cargo steamship and sailing ship services combined with the development of the railways to make both urgent and profitable the construction of new and improved harbours, jetties and piers'. Morecambe was a classic example of plans for a junction of railways and a new port leading to the almost accidental establishment of a seaside town. Ramsgate, Gravesend, Margate and Southend benefited directly from improvements in shipping and their attraction for Londoners was enhanced because of the relative swiftness of the new steamboats which plied down the Thames. When Dickens's Tuggs family (in *Sketches by Boz*) inherited a small fortune, they immediately turned their thoughts to leaving their London shop.

> Everyone concurred that this was an indispensable preliminary to being genteel. The question then arose – Where should they go?
> 'Gravesend,' mildly suggested Mr Joseph Tuggs. The idea was universally scouted. Gravesend was *low*.
> 'Margate,' insinuated Mrs Tuggs. Worse and worse – nobody there but tradespeople.
> 'Brighton!'

The Brighton route had, however, seen too many accidents recently; the Tuggs finally opted for Ramsgate. Two months later

> the City of London Ramsgate steamer was running gaily down the river. Her flag was flying, her band was playing, her passengers were conversing; everything about her seemed gay and lively. – No wonder – The Tuggs's were on board.

The technical improvements in maritime engineering produced a proliferation of one particular form of Victorian architecture which has to this day characterized English seaside resorts – the pier. In origin, piers were purely functional, being built out to sea to provide a safe and efficient landing place for ships docking at a coastal town which lacked a natural harbour or safe anchorage. Both Margate and Yarmouth had piers to cope with coastal traffic as early as 1800, but it was the improvements in the use of metals and new engineering techniques, allied to the upsurge in shipping, which demanded more than mere stone or wooden jetties laid across the beach. In time the new iron constructions were themselves to become central attractions of seaside towns, and local authorities and investors rushed to erect new piers, even when the resort had no shipping to speak of. And a number of resorts, not satisfied with a single pier, created more, as competing groups sought to capitalize on the piers' attractions.

Fittingly, Brighton had the first important metal pier – the famous Chain Pier, opened in 1823. Designed by a naval engineer, Samuel Brown, the pier incorporated bold design and the most advanced thought on suspension bridges. (Brown had discussed the design with Thomas Telford, then at work on the Menai Straits bridge.) Its purpose was utilitarian – to provide for the frequent ships, particularly the cross-Channel vessels calling at Brighton – but the boldness of its engineering, and the appeal of its Egyptian towers, rapidly established the Chain Pier as an independent attraction, even in a town of unusual and graceful architecture. Two years later, the first steamships began to sail to Brighton and the pier's usefulness was vindicated. Brighton's example was clear to all and there was further grist to the pier-builder's mill when, following the opening of Southend's pier for steamships in 1830, the town experienced an upsurge in visitors from London. By 1830, Brighton and Southend had shown the economic virtues of the pier. Piers, like the resorts they came to represent, were creations of the march of industry and progress. Soon the piers themselves were further transformed into places of fun which offered lucrative investment for their owners and backers.

Victorian piers were designed to be attractive, utilizing enterprising methods of cast-iron construction, though by the late century, both pier-building and the entertainments the piers came to house, had become standardized. Though many are battered, derelict, modernized or blighted, some fifty-four remain today as monuments to the Victorian resorts. The piers involved, however, a considerable capital outlay. Blackpool's North Pier, opened in 1863, cost a hefty £13,500. Southend's famous pier cost £42,000. Brighton's West Pier, opened in 1866, cost £30,000. But the financiers had made a shrewd investment, for Victorian holiday-makers headed for the piers as surely as they headed for the beach. One Sunday, some 10,000 paid to stroll along Brighton's West Pier; in 1875 alone, more than 600,000 people had paid at the turnstiles.

By the 1860s piers had fully established themselves as independent attractions of the seaside resorts and no resort worthy of the name could be without one. They were unusual and distinctive objects of the shoreline, allowing Victorian visitors a sense of venturing out to sea while remaining on *terra firma*. And as steamers began to ply between the resorts – or even around the bay – the piers made it possible for the seaside visitors to enjoy trips out to sea. Late in the century, under the patronage of the Prince of Wales, there developed a cult of sailing, and the piers and the boats which docked there allowed even the poor visitors a glimpse of a world reserved for their social betters.

The urban growth of the resorts involved more than the proliferation of hotels and houses, for perhaps the major problem facing the resorts was how to keep the sea at bay. At many resorts it was obvious that some form of bulwark was needed against the high tides, floods and storms. As a result sea-walls were constructed and it is interesting that even they came to be utilized for leisure, for they provided a firm roadway for walking or riding along. Gradually the seaside promenade, like the piers, became a feature of the resorts, though this was particularly the case where towns developed initially along the line of the coast. In 1841, Dr Granville noted of Blackpool that 'the colony is travelling southward' and this linear development was equally noticeable at Southend and, later, Bournemouth. The consequences of such development were profound, for, as Professor Gilbert has noted, it resulted in the urban encroachment on mile after mile of coastline. Defending the seashore by walls and promenades was an inevitable consequence of the growth of seaside towns and meant that the visitors were increasingly subjected to an urban environment, though one which, by being perched on the water's edge, seemed quite different from inland towns.

Yet the thousands of visitors who went to resorts in the years 1840–60, and who enjoyed the increasingly refined and urban facilities of the seaside, were limited in many respects. The chief difficulties facing potential visitors, particularly among the lower income groups, were the economic and social restraints of urban, industrial life. For rural workers these restraints were even more severe and, except where they lived close to the sea, agricultural folk were to be much slower than town-dwellers in enjoying visits to the seaside on a regular basis. For industrial working men and their families the resorts – opened up by the railway excursion – remained tantalizingly distant, for though the trains undoubtedly brought the sea closer, the rigours of industrial life, with its long hours, low and often uncertain income and few holidays, provided few opportunities for extended or even regular visits to the coast. Seaside holidays like other forms of leisure in mid Victorian England, had been dangled before thousands of people who could scarcely afford them. And yet the development of the railways had shown the potential for mass leisure at the seaside, just as it had shown the possibility of nationwide organized sports. But as long as the great majority of urban people remained shackled to unrewarding and time-consuming work, the potential of travel – to the seaside or elsewhere – and of leisure and popular culture, would continue to thrive and prosper primarily as a local phenomenon. What was needed was a little more money and free time before working people could fully benefit from the facilities of the railways – and the seaside resorts.

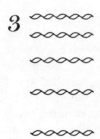

⚬⚬⚬⚬⚬ In pre-industrial England there had been a recognizable holiday calendar which for the poor had punctuated their round of labour and toil. The major breaks from work were days of religious significance – Easter, Christmas and Whitsuntide – though there was a complexity of feasts, fairs and wakes, often on a local, parish basis, which reflected the rhythms and patterns of agricultural life. In rural communities these breaks from work, with their own complex cultural forms, continued well into and beyond the years of industrialization. But for that new species of people, industrial workers, whose lives in these same years were increasingly shaped by an urban environment, memories and survivals of rurally based recreations slipped to the back of their distant memories, as industry came to demand of them complete and relatively unbending commitment. In the heavy industries which formed the backbone of the first industrial revolution, the men, women and children who were transformed into 'hands' were, in general, purged of their rights to leisure. Moreover, the denial of leisure to early industrial workers was not simply an accidental function of an impersonal uncontrollable system; it was encouraged and perfected by those captains of industry for whom time was money. Lost time meant lost money, an equation all the more beguiling following the widespread and expensive introduction of the steam engine in the textile industry. The new industries were synonymous with excessive hours of work – excessive not merely by modern standards but also by contemporary ones. What appalled Englishmen was the apparent encouragement of such long hours of work. 'The pronounced tendency of this age to utilitarianism,' wrote the Rev. Martin in 1863, 'and the worship of wealth acting on the energy and earnestness natural to the English character, have resulted in the establishment of a highly artificial system of over-working which excludes re-creation.'

Time and again, socially conscious observers were as ap-palled by the deliberate denial of leisure rights, as they were by the more mechanical consequences of industrialization. Many were convinced of the success of 'high and influential persons' in trying 'to curb, restrain and almost absolutely forbid the lowly and humble from indulging in any pastimes whatso-ever'.

In the teeth of industrial conditions which eroded traditional holidays and inflicted a punitive working week on all and sundry, conceding free time only on Sundays, Christmas, Easter and Whitsuntide, it was impossible for many working people to enjoy a number of readily available recreations. Despite the efficiency of the railway system in the 1840s, until working hours were reduced, the prospects of recreational travel for many working people were slim – especially when Sunday travel was so contested.

The cotton industry exemplified industrialization, and in-evitably it was there, with its heavy concentration of female and child labour, that industrial problems were seen at their worst. From the early days there had been determined attempts to introduce legislation to curb the worst excesses and secure some free time from work. Acts in 1802, 1819, 1825, 1829, 1831 and 1833 produced piecemeal and haphazard improvements in factory conditions, but hours of work remained arduous, and committees throughout the industrial north sprang up to press for shorter hours. 'Short Time Committees' campaigned throughout the 1830s and 1840s for a reduction in the working week, concentrating on a demand first made by Manchester cotton operatives in 1818 for a ten-and-a-half-hour day. Two men in particular helped to establish these claims in the years after 1830 – a Yorkshire manufacturer, John Wood, and Richard Oastler, who invested his campaign with a strong religious overtone. Supported in Parliament by the radical Tory John Hobhouse, Oastler's efforts – and those of working people themselves – slowly eroded parliamentary and industrial resistance. Cutting across party divides, the parliamentary drive for shorter hours produced a bizarre mixture of political alignments; but gradually numbers of factory owners came to see the benefits to be derived from shorter hours.

The central thrust of arguments for a shorter working week centred on the need to protect women and children, but the male labouring force undoubtedly used these more appealing 'humanitarian' arguments to force home their own case. Throughout, partisan evidence from embryonic unions, interested parties and commissions flew off the presses and in 1833 a new Act further limited working hours in the textile trades. But there was a plethora of other industries where conditions were no less arduous, and renewed agitation, stemming from the shocking evidence in the mines, helped in 1844 to produce limitations on their hours of work. It was not until 1850, though, that further improvements secured the end of work on Saturday afternoon. Work was to stop at 2 p.m. on Saturday – a move establishing 'la semaine anglaise' and offering a precedent for all other industrial workers in succeeding years.

Legislation was of course only one way of making such gains, and in many industries, particularly where the labour force was highly concentrated and therefore easily organized, negotiations with ownership and management produced free Saturday afternoons by voluntary agreements. In one industry after another the work-force insisted on limiting the working day and securing a free Saturday afternoon. But because these concessions came slowly and on an industrial and often regional basis, the evolution of the distinctively free Saturday afternoon was slow, fragmentary and uneven.

Following the success of the textile industry, in 1852–6 the Birmingham engineering trades gradually won free Saturday afternoons. Slowly the concession spread to other cities, though much depended on the nature of local industry and the state of local prosperity, In Liverpool, for example, despite the efforts of the local 'Saturday Half-Time Association', the weekly break came late. Enjoyed by the local engineering élite in the 1850s, it did not reach other skilled workers until the 1870s and finally reached the unskilled only in the last twenty years of the century. A similar slow process could be seen at work in other trades and cities. In London, for example, the building trade secured a 4 p.m. end to work in 1847; by 1861 it was reduced to 2 p.m., and, in 1871, reduced still further to 1 p.m. But among the engineers in the north-east of England, as late as 1890, a major demand remained that work should cease at one o'clock on Saturdays. Overall, however, the cumulative process resulted in the slow erosion throughout Victorian England of the hours of work in industry, so much so that, when in 1897 the Webbs were discussing working hours in *Industrial Democracy*, they took eight hours to be 'The Natural Day'.

The long-term consequences of limiting the working week were profound. Clearly the most important result was a move towards ending, in heavy industries at least, an industrial regime which corroded health, destroyed working-class industrial leisure and was economically counter-productive. But a major secondary result was the gradual releasing of more and more industrial workers for leisure; they were given free time to spend as they wanted. No longer were they restricted to Sundays and infrequent national or local holidays – and hence shackled to the religious whims of transport owners or the effectiveness of Sabbatarian pressure groups. Saturday was their day and it soon became the national day for mass leisure, exemplified by the growth of football as a game of working men. Thomas Wright, a Manchester working man who rose to fame in the mid century, succinctly described the importance of Saturday to working people:

> It is now a stock saying with many working men, that *Saturday* is the best day of the week, as it is a short working day, and Sunday has to come . . . When the bell rings the men leave the works in a leisurely way that contrasts rather strongly with the eagerness with which they leave at other times; but once outside the workshop gates, the younger apprentices and other boys immediately devote themselves to the business of pleasure.

Furthermore, in many industries the ending of Saturday afternoon work coincided with an increased spending power in certain groups. This was not of course prosperity in any recognizable modern form. But it *did* mean that some working people were able to save small amounts for other than the necessities of life – and they also had a little more time in which to spend it.

Free time and spare cash were slowly reshaping the face of English leisure and recreation.

From mid century, England was passing out of that first painful phase of industrialization – from an epoch in which dislocation and harshness had characterized the lives of the first industrial labour force – into the third quarter of the century in which, according to Pollard and Crossley, 'the bulk of the working classes, and particularly the factory workers and the skilled workers, were at last beginning to get some of the benefits of industrialization.' The years after the Crystal Palace Exhibition of 1851 have traditionally been offered as a turning-point. Mid Victorian prosperity was most noticeable among the burgeoning middle class. But even in working-class circles the signs of better times litter the historical records, and few improvements were more obvious, striking – and pleasurable – than the trips to the seaside which working people increasingly enjoyed as the century progressed.

Organized leisure required money as much as free time and it is noticeable that those groups able to improve working conditions also benefited financially. Cotton and building workers experienced a sharp rise in wages in the third quarter of the century – faster even than other skilled men (printers, engineers and shipbuilders, for instance). And on the whole these skilled groups were able to maintain their wage differentials over the unskilled. The formula looks crude but seductively simple: those with strong unions benefited while those without slipped back. And among the latter – unskilled and unorganized – poverty, unemployment and old age continued to work their traditionally harrowing results. Mayhew stands as a monumental reminder to any glib generalization we might offer about improving conditions. Nonetheless, substantial numbers of working people enjoyed better times as the century advanced.

Nowhere was this more obvious than in savings habits. By mid century Friendly Societies had 1½ million depositors – the very great majority from the working class; by 1873 a further 1½ million people saved in the Savings Bank and a similar number in the newly established Post Office Savings Bank. In these last two, perhaps one third of depositors were working men, and when these figures are added to the savers in the trade unions and co-operative societies, it becomes clear that the habit of saving money had established itself as a major social force among working people by about 1875. Thrift as an individual or collective virtue was clearly not *created* in the years 1850–75, for it was only the most careful and parsimonious rationing of scarce resources which had kept lower-class families together in the bleak first phase of industrialization (and continued to among the poor). But the working-class virtues of thrift and carefulness were, in the third quarter of the century, able to yield more obvious results. For many working people, the inevitable indebtedness of their parents and grandparents gave way to a limited, and often precarious, solvency. Spare money was, by the 1870s, not simply the monopoly of the middle and upper classes. And the degree to which leisure patterns were changing in these years is perhaps the best indicator of this fact. Working-class Saturday afternoons, with their football, summer excursions or even the simpler, but nonetheless important, habits of regular shopping, provide tangible and increasingly commonplace proof of the existence of a new, though limited, working-class consumer power.

From the 1850s onwards contemporaries were struck by the rising potential for mass leisure as free time and spare money were releasing significant numbers of people for leisure pursuits. Among the middle and upper classes, there was deep concern that this free time should be used by working men for self-education and improvement. Local men of substance subsequently sought to provide 'useful recreations' which would both amuse and educate. In 1846 the *General Advertiser* was founded as 'a journal of literature, Science and Art, and the advocate of an abridgement of the hours of business in all trades with a view to the physical, intellectual, and moral improvement of the Industrial Classes'. When, two years earlier, merchants in Manchester had granted a Saturday half-holiday to their employees, they published a *Half-Holiday Handbook*, 'with a view to supplying a source to which the numerous class . . . may resort for a guide to excursions and rambles'. Within a decade the volume of mass popular leisure in the major cities was quite staggering, ranging from concerts in town halls, the opening of new municipal parks, through to Liverpool and London river steamers regularly filled with weekend crowds.

By the mid 1850s it was obvious that regular breaks from

work were beneficial for working people; nor did they undermine industrial profitability. The feeling grew that free time and holidays ought perhaps to be provided on a more organized and rational basis for, despite the spread of free Saturday afternoons, holidays continued to be enjoyed primarily on the old, traditional days of rest. Writing in 1868, Thomas Wright 'The Journeyman Engineer' noted:

> Many of the unwashed now participate in the benefits of the Saturday half-holiday movement; – others indulge more or less in the worship of Saint Monday; and in some districts there are occasional holidays in connection with local customs. These, however, are but partial or accidental holidays, and the holidays proper of the unwashed are the three great festivals of Christmas, Easter, and Whitsuntide. Of these, Easter, viewed purely as a holiday, is the greatest.

What made such holidays possible was the habit of 'saving up'. 'Even in their pleasures, those of the working classes who would enjoy them thoroughly must be provident; must "save up" for them – provide for their *sunny* as well as rainy days.' Moreover, much of the pleasure of Easter and Whitsuntide breaks, unlike Christmas which tended to be a family affair, was the sense of mass participation. It was a massive, communal bolt for the fresh air, and the resorts and parks steeled themselves for the expected invasions of city-dwellers. In June 1865 *The Times* carried advertisements for a number of special Whitsuntide excursions to the coast and, for the better off, even to Calais.

But these breaks were exceptional and there were countless people who remained immovably rooted to their homes or jobs. Holidays – at home, to say nothing of excursions to the coast – were something about which millions may have dreamed but which they scarcely ever enjoyed. Nowhere was this more clearly the case than with agricultural workers, that diffuse and oppressed body of people whose condition in mid Victorian England was so depressed. When, late in the century, their lot improved slightly, it left little cash available for the luxuries of holidays (which in any case could only be enjoyed on Sundays).

Within the towns and cities there were large groups of workers who similarly failed to enjoy the benefits of holidays, especially in the new areas of economic growth which created thousands of clerical and office jobs lacking in industrial protection. Armies of clerks, office workers, shop workers and women in the sweated trades were created by changes in the economy. The 217,000 people in commercial occupations in 1871, for example, had grown to 896,000 by 1911. The revolution in retailing, with its proliferation of shops, chain-stores and high-street outlets, produced an equally striking upsurge in new shop workers. And all these groups tended to work excessively long hours for extremely poor wages.

Whereas workers in the traditional industries had powerful voices to speak for them, who was there to stand up for these 'new' workers – and for the legions of domestics hidden by the exploitative formality of life in middle- and upper-class households? When mid Victorians spoke of the exploitation of labour, they frequently referred to the abject condition of people 'in service'. According to the *Edinburgh Review* of April 1862, there had been 'a great revival of that particular grievance which every generation laments, denounces, and perpetuates – the grievance arising out of the conditions of domestic service, and the class of domestic servants'. A decade later, similar complaints regularly found their way into the English press. 'The hardest worked class of women are domestic servants, especially in schools, hotels and lodging houses . . . On Saturday, the factory-hand works two hours less than usual. The housemaid, on the contrary, works harder. On Sunday, the factory-hand and the shopwoman rest completely; the housemaid only partially.' Without an organization, it was clear that the interests of these people could be safeguarded only by Parliament itself. And it was to be in Parliament, in a drive to provide relief for such workers, that a major and distinctively English piece of reform was made in the provision of holidays.

Non-unionized workers found an unlikely champion in the person of Sir John Lubbock (later Lord Avebury) who, on being elected to Parliament, declared his intention 'to secure some holidays and some shortening of hours for the most hardly worked classes of the community'. Lubbock was concerned about the disparities in facilities and opportunities for leisure between different groups of working people, arguing quite forcefully against those whose holidays were already secured: 'Artisans do not need another holiday so much as others less fortunately situated. They have secured for themselves short (I do not say too short) hours and a weekly half-holiday. The so-called working man, in fact, works less than almost any other class of the community.'

Blaming Puritan England for the loss of many ancient holidays (though in fact industrialization had accounted for many more), Lubbock pointed out that whereas most people enjoyed Easter and Whit Monday, Boxing Day, Christmas Day and Good Friday, employees in banks were guaranteed only Christmas Day and Good Friday. Lubbock therefore set himself the task of implementing legislation to extend the holidays of bank employees and others in similar restricted occupations. His main problem was not the resistance of vested-interest groups, but the banks' hours and times of business. Bills of exchange, drawable on one of the rare holidays (or Sunday), were customarily cashed by the banks on the day before the holiday. Lubbock therefore proposed that such transactions should be payable instead on the day *after* a holiday. And to devise a special name for the resulting extra day's holiday, Lubbock hit upon the term 'Bank Holiday', a happy accident which prevented the growth of opposition to the new Bill. 'If we had called our Bill the "General Holiday Bill" or the "National Holiday Bill", I doubt not that it would have been opposed.' Lubbock denied that this provision was made specially for bank employees, for it 'expressly enacts that no person shall be compelled to do anything on a Bank Holiday which he could not be compelled to do on Christmas Day or Good Friday.'

The Bank Holiday – its passage through Parliament secured by its accidentally deceptive title – became a fact of national life as soon as it was enacted in 1871. Lubbock's highest hopes were reserved for the August Bank Holiday: 'I have always expected that the first Monday in August, coming as it does in the glory of summer, would eventually become the most popular holiday of the year.' But even Lubbock could scarcely have envisaged the amazing scenes of popular recreation which promptly greeted the new Act. It was immediately obvious that this simple piece of legislation had tapped the enormous national potential for leisure. The English people took to roads, rail and steamers in their millions. Looking out from London, *The Times* reported that

> cyclists of both sexes covered the roads. River steamers and pleasure boats carried their thousands to Kew and the upper reaches of the Thames. The London parks were crowded. The Botanic Gardens and Zoological Gardens formed great attractions, and the flowers of Battersea Park drew large crowds all day. The India and Ceylon Exhibition was visited by an enormous crowd.

But it was the railway system which bore the full brunt of the Bank Holiday traffic – and continued to do so until the arrival of motor transport in the twentieth century. The *News of the World* vividly captured the scenes on that first August Bank Holiday in 1871.

> From 8 a.m. the cry at every railway station was 'Still they come!' and the supply of passengers very far exceeded the supply of accommodation. At Fenchurch St Station there was a crowd of hundreds struggling for tickets to Margate and Southend . . . The passengers were packed on decks and paddle-boxes like herrings in a barrel . . . Margate Jetty was simply blocked so far as to be impassable, whilst thousands of excursionists who came down by rail wandered along the cliffs. How many may have gone down it is impossible to say. The people arrived at Cannon St and Charing Cross for Ramsgate at 8 a.m., and it was 10 o'clock before the surprised but very active officials of the South Eastern could accommodate all their customers. Seven 'specials' were sent from Cannon St, and probably as many more from Highgate Hill. It was simply impossible to get to the seaside.

Some people, unable to get to the coast, switched directions and headed, by train or boat, up the Thames. But there, so severe was the unexpected pressure on taverns and shops that beer and tobacco ran out. On all sides, people openly put down their good fortunes in enjoying the holiday to Sir John Lubbock, and according to the *News of the World* 'his great reputation as a man of science has been enhanced by the invention of Bank Holidays . . . he has added – substantially added – to the sum of human happiness, and has carried rays of hope and joy into

humble households so great as to rank high as a public benefactor.'

Such fulsome praise was repeated time and again, both by
the revellers on the day itself, and in the popular press over the
following days. *Bell's Life* noted:

> Thus has a real and unqualified summer holiday blossomed
> into existence, and it may be said the only one we have, for
> the other escape days are in spring and winter. This holiday
> is, indeed, an outer (an out-and-outer), as Christmas Day
> may be considered a family fire-side festival.

There was of course an element of curiosity and unique excitement about the very first Bank Holiday, but the second break,
in 1872, confirmed all the predictions of the first. And, again,
popular approval was bestowed on the by now universally
famous Lubbock. 'All other popularity in arms, arts, song or
statesmanship', wrote the *Daily Telegraph*, 'was as nothing on
Monday last compared to that of Sir John Lubbock.' The universal effectiveness of the August Holiday was staggering,
'and so general is the disposition to make holiday that an enterprising pawnbroker thinks it needful to advertise that his
establishment will remain open'. The *Daily News* commented
that:

> This statute holiday gives a day in the fresh summer air –
> and let us hope in the summer sunshine – to tens of thousands
> of persons who might otherwise altogether miss the sight of
> the yellow corn-fields or the summer woods.

In the words of Mr Pooter, that absurd snob whose lowly clerical
job induced aspirations towards the style of his superiors,
'August 13th. Hurrah! at Broadstairs.'

During the ensuing quarter of a century, the August Bank
Holiday became a distinctive feature of the English summer, and
the railways provided full scope for the thousands of trippers
who left the cities for the coast, country and holiday retreats.
Many of course resented the unleashing of the 'poorer sorts' on
to resorts where middle-class visitors had ensconced themselves
for the summer. One visitor to Teignmouth complained in 1888,
'On a universal holiday the shops everywhere are all closed,

while the poor railwaymen get overworked, and there is greater risk of accidents, owing to the multitude which travel.'

Critics took what were in fact the very successes of the Bank Holiday – the releasing of previously shackled working people – as evidence of the legislation's failure. The statistical evidence was overwhelming, however – as was popular approval for 'St Lubbock's Day'. By the mid 1890s the number leaving London's stations for the coast and country was approaching the half-million mark; visitors to the parks and museums in and around London were calculated at 360,000. Given the sheer pressure of such numbers, the uprooting of armies of people from restricted, daily routines and the fact that they were deposited far from home in a carnival atmosphere, it is not surprising that accusations of drunkenness and unruly behaviour were levelled at the Bank Holidays. But, generally, such accusations were unfounded and evidence suggested that drunkenness and related crimes actually declined on the Bank Holidays.

By the turn of the century, Rowntree discovered that, even among the local poor in York (his 'Group D'), 'During the August Bank Holiday week, working men from York crowd into Scarborough, and many of those who do not take such an extended holiday avail themselves of cheap day and half-day excursions run by the North-East Company.' On receiving news of the relief of Mafeking in May 1900, the Lord Mayor of York declared a local holiday and, as a result, according to the local newspaper reports, 'the citizens were abroad in great numbers. Many determined to utilise their freedom from the daily round by going off to the seaside or into the country, and the morning trains have borne away a considerable proportion of these pleasure seekers.' The seaside habit was similar elsewhere. In 1903 Charles Booth, reflecting on his survey of London's poor, found evidence from contemporaries that 'holiday making is spoken of as "one of the most remarkable changes in habit in the last ten years" and the statement is applicable to all classes.'

In Hackney, a clergyman reported that 'the district is almost deserted on Bank Holiday. The women go off as well as the men.' One observer thought that such holidays were instrumental in drawing people away from the public house.

Employees, however, tended to extend the holiday simply by staying away from work on the days after the Bank Holiday, a fact bemoaned by employers. 'It is useless to open the works on the day after Bank Holiday, or even for two days.' Among such men the Bank Holidays were regarded as a curse, compounded by the lack of restraint which seemed to characterize people enjoying themselves *en masse*. But like it or not, witnesses had to admit that by the turn of the century the ordinary people of London had begun to ask a new question of life around them. 'To "what shall we eat, what drink, and wherewithal shall we be clothed?" must now be added the question, "How shall we be amused?" '

In fact, the evidence is confusing. General Booth of the Salvation Army offered quite a different view: 'Notwithstanding the cheapest rates and frequent excursions, there are multitudes of the poor who, year in and out, never get beyond the crowded city.' But it is revealing that Booth sought to remedy this by creating 'Whitechapel-by-the-Sea' for the urban poor. It is clear that a trip to the seaside had become a commonplace aspiration, if not a reality, among England's city-dwellers. By the late years of the nineteenth century, enjoyments on an organized, mass scale had become a feature of urban life. Fun, as an aspect of material consumption, was an integral part of life – among working people as well as their betters – and it could be found in music-halls, brass-bands, football teams and pub life. Above all, it was seen in the Bank Holiday excursions to the seaside.

4 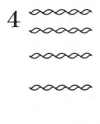 *Life at the Seaside*

⌒⌒⌒⌒⌒ By the 1860s the English seaside resorts had, largely through the changing economic climate, which brought the formerly upper- and middle-class holidaying habit within the reach of others, become a major fact of English social life. Manufacturers and retailers (always a good index to a society's changing fancies) eagerly seized on this fact and began to produce goods specifically for seaside life. Peter Robinson, for example, offered yachting and special 'seaside' jackets, H. J. and D. Nicholl of Regent Street advertised serge, tweed and cloth 'Promenade Costumes', and in 1867 the 'Great Shawl and Cloak Emporium' announced the 'Atlantic Yachting Suit', a 'very durable and pretty suit for Seaside Wear'. But in the 1860s such goods could scarcely appeal to working people who, whatever their early gains from a new phase of industrialization, were still hard-pressed simply to keep themselves solvent. Seaside clothes were clearly designed for the upper- and middle-class markets.

By the mid years of the century, the Victorian middle class – bigger, more acquisitive and more confident than ever – were anxious to enjoy the extended delights of seaside holidays. And they were encouraged to do so, not simply because of their burgeoning prosperity but also because prevailing medical and cultural orthodoxy saw in the resorts an excellent antidote to the dangers and illnesses endemic in the towns. It was of course poor town-dwellers who were in greatest need of a break by the sea, but the English middle class also found sound reasons for subjecting themselves to the coast's bracing air. And while medical opinion continued to promote the seaside, by the 1860s it did so for new reasons. A century before, Dr Russell had recommended the water; henceforth, doctors began to recommend the air, for by mid century medical opinion came to regard the sea air as the seaside's chief attraction, and even began to qualify older recommendations for seabathing.

Writing in 1860, Dr Spencer Thomson laid down a severe regime for potential bathers, recommending no more than twenty minutes at the longest and no bathing before breakfast or after meals – strictures which would have bemused medical men a century before. In 1798, for example, a Scarborough man had suggested, 'For those who are robust, the morning, before breakfast, is the best time; for those who are delicate, it may be better to take breakfast first.' The drift of Dr Thomson's argument against seabathing was so severe that he felt obliged to apologize to his readers: 'Do not suppose that we are writing an indiscriminate condemnation of sea-bathing. Nothing of the kind.' But, despite his denials, readers of his book, searching for medical advice on seaside resorts would have found precious little inducement to swim in the sea in comparison with the way Englishmen had been urged to the water's edge by their doctors over the past century.

Dr Thomson suggested less demanding forms of seaside invigoration: 'In short, sea air is eminently possessed of those properties which tend to stimulate, and to give a healthy character to the blood, and through it . . . to the entire bodily system.' Thomson consequently set himself the task of providing a health-seeker's guide to the resorts, and again and again he returned to the resorts' climate rather than the sea water. Like any respectable Victorian gentleman, however, Thomson was equally concerned with the social *tone* of the resorts, for a town's undoubted medical virtues could be undermined by social factors. Social class could determine a town's attraction as much as its water or bracing air. Margate, called by some: 'low, *bourgeois*', was adequate, 'if you are a tired Londoner, not too dignified or distingué'. Ramsgate attracted visitors who 'seem to have no more sense of decency than so many South-Sea Islanders'. Broadstairs, on the other hand, was ideal for anyone in search of peace and quiet, and, while Brighton had still remained 'that queen of the sea-coast towns', it had 'been converted into a marine suburb of London by the iron rail'. But it was to the health-giving values of the resorts that

Thomson directed his attention, and his emphasis upon climate and the sea air was easily translated into practice along the promenades and piers. When, in 1861, a group of Blackpool townsmen met to discuss provision for 'greater promenading space of the most invigorating kind', it was agreed to 'erect a substantial and safe means for the visitors to walk over the sea at a distance of thirteen hundred and fifty feet at high water'.

Predictably, doctors tended to stress the value of their own town's atmosphere. In 1869 Dr Oliver of Redcar wrote: 'How well Redcar is adapted to the debilitated class of invalids, not only by reason of its powerfully tonic atmosphere and excellent bathing but because of the natural facilities afforded by its extensive beach for easy exercise.' Such emphasis on the atmosphere rather than the water recurs throughout mid- and late-nineteenth-century literature on the seaside and, to a large extent, it reflected the understandable Victorian obsession with pulmonary complaints. Tuberculosis was, in nineteenth-century Britain, a killing disease which accounted for one death in six, and it flourished in the overcrowded cities, particularly among the undernourished and overworked. Like poverty itself, T.B. hit the most abject most severely but it was not, of course, a respecter of class and it made fearful ravages among city-dwellers of all social stations. The knowledge that T.B. was primarily an urban disease encouraged those who were able to flee – regularly, for the whole summer, or, in the case of the prosperous, on a permanent basis – to travel to the coast where, at least, their lungs could be filled with fresh air.

Although it is true that the incidence of T.B. was lowered as the century advanced (particularly after the discovery in 1882 of the tubercle bacillus carried in milk), this disease became the social equivalent of cholera and typhoid. A Royal Commission as late as 1908 called it 'the most pauperising of all diseases'. Six years later, part of Lloyd George's drive for National Health Insurance was directed against the 'terrible scourge of consumption'. From the early nineteenth century, fresh air had been thought suitable for a variety of urban diseases, and one hospital for London sufferers of scrofula was opened at Margate as early as 1800. But the medical establishment frowned upon the belief that T.B. could itself be helped by fresh air and, as late as 1840, the *Lancet* continued to attack those who advocated such treatment. In the 1850s, however, research in Germany firmly supported the physical benefits of fresh air for T.B. patients, particularly at high altitudes. Medical opinion swung quickly into line, encouraging the movement of T.B. patients to the coast. Medicine, again, reinforced social custom in approving of the coastal resorts. To be beside the seaside was, for millions, pure enjoyment; for many others it meant the difference between life and death – or at worst, a prolonging of a troubled life.

Throughout the century, therefore, the seaside towns offered an escape and, hopefully, a respite from Victorian pulmonary complaints; often, too, the seaside became the last resting place of victims of those diseases. For the more prosperous, the lakes and mountains of Britain and Europe seemed an even greater attraction. In fact, the appeal of the English Lakes and the Scottish Highlands had been established in the late eighteenth century by the same social forces which had shaped the emergence of the seaside resorts. William Wilberforce, in search of solitude and peace, had rented a house at Windermere in 1781, but gave it up seven years later: 'The Tour to the Lakes has become so fashionable that the banks of the Thames are scarcely more public than those of Windermere.' The fashionable search for inland beauty – in part a function of early Romanticism – was encouraged by the travel books of the Rev. William Gilpin. Inevitably, perhaps, such works were swiftly and vigorously ridiculed by the caricaturists. Nonetheless, such inland tours were commonplace by the early nineteenth century and were further encouraged by the 'popularization' of the seaside resorts and the growing medical emphasis on the benefits of fresh air, a process that was hastened by the spread of the railways to Windermere and into the Highlands. Nor did the Queen's obsession with Balmoral undermine upper-class interest in the Highlands. 'Every year,' she wrote, 'my heart becomes more fixed in this dear Paradise and so much more so now, that *all* has become my dearest Albert's *own* creation, own work, own building.' Scotland reminded Albert of Germany, and he felt less alien there than in England. Predictably, many of those upper-class people able to afford the cost, followed their monarch north of the border for their holidays and retreats.

Many Victorians sought better health in the mountains of Europe. Conan Doyle took his consumptive wife to Davos in the 1860s (and found inspiration for Moriarty), and Robert Louis Stevenson also sought a restoration of good health there. Indeed, the escape to mountain retreats by consumptive Victorians became a cause, an occasion and an inspiration for an abundance of European literature, best remembered perhaps in Thomas Mann's *Magic Mountain*. By late century, the virtues of mountain air were widely accepted by those able to travel to Europe. But, for many more people, the English seaside offered a more practical escape. 'The restorative properties of sea air have long been fully appreciated,' wrote Dr Yeo in 1882, 'although regular and periodical migrations to the seashore is a custom of modern origin.' Increasingly, then, Victorians turned to the coast for rest, health, pleasure or simply out of awe-struck curiosity, in the case of those for whom a day at the seaside was the height of worldly enjoyment.

Whatever the inducement or recommendation not to swim, whatever the motive for visiting the seaside, the sea itself remained a main attraction in mid century. In August 1860 *The Times* commented: 'Down comes the Excursion Train, with its thousands – some with a month's range, others tethered to a six hours' limit, but all rushing with one impulse to the water's edge.' Such popularity was not universally approved, for Victorian resorts touched a number of exposed Victorian sensitivities about morality and personal conduct. Worse even than the desecration of the Lord's Day, in the eyes of many Victorians, was the state of abandoned nudity so commonplace at English resorts. What French resorts boldly proclaim in the 1970s, a century before had been a common sight on English beaches. The reasons were simple; for until the emergence of mass-produced bathing-costumes later in the century, swimming garments were either unheard-of or too expensive, and much too cumbersome for comfort. Swimmers, particularly the men, consequently took the plunge in the nude.

Dr Thomson felt obliged to warn visitors to the coast: 'One more word upon the almost heathen indecency of our sea-bathing places . . . In most places but Britain, male bathers are compelled to wear some sort of decent covering, such as short drawers . . . the present indecency is not diminished by the un-blushing intrusiveness of some of the fair sex.' Not everyone agreed, however. For example, the Rev. Francis Kilvert, who plunged into the sea whenever he visited the seaside, confided in his diary in June 1874:

At Shanklin one has to adopt the detestable custom of bathing in drawers. If ladies don't like to see men naked why don't they keep away from the sight? Today I had a pair of drawers given me which I could not keep on. The rough waves stripped them off and tore them down round my ankles.

For Kilvert and his kind there was, however, the advantage that nude bathing gave him the opportunity of seeing naked females in the water. In July 1875, again at the Isle of Wight, Kilvert recorded:

One beautiful girl stood entirely naked on the sand, and there as she sat, half reclined sideways, leaning upon her elbow with her knee bent and her legs and feet partly drawn back and up, she was a model for a sculptor, there was a supple slender waist, the gentle dawn and tender swell of the bosom and the budding breasts, the graceful rounding of the delicately beautiful limbs and above all the soft exquisite curves of the rosy dimpled bottom and broad white thighs.

For such sexually frustrated Victorian gentlemen, the seaside must have provided rare erotic experiences (although it is fair to add that Kilvert's diaries reflect a man who was obsessed with eroticism).

Public bathing undoubtedly troubled lots of Victorians; they worried about the dressing and undressing, the segregation of the sexes in the sea and on the beaches, and of course they fretted about the attire of the swimmers. The whole exercise seemed, as it attracted more and more participants in the last twenty years of the century, an indelicate exercise in exhibitionism which required firm control. At Torquay William Miller was shocked to see 'a number of working men (it was Saturday afternoon) [who] whisked off their clothes at the wall on the beach and ran like savages to the water.' Even at Bournemouth, that 'fashionable health resort', nude bathing was commonplace, made worse in Miller's eyes by the mixing of the sexes: 'The forwardness of the women makes it unpleasant for the bathers.

For not content with gazing down from the cliffs above . . .
they are often passing by or near the bathers . . . I think the
visitors to Bournemouth are more shameless than at any other
place.' At Yarmouth, Miller was struck by female swimming-
costumes: 'Many of the ladies appeared to fancy the tight-
fitting pink bathing-dress – perhaps because of its resemblance
to the human colour, though more probably because of its
brightness.' At Ramsgate, the sea 'was filled with a heap of
mingled pale-faced and rosy nymphs in scanty and dripping
attire, and all sorts of little cockneys . . . sans gloves, sans
well-brushed hat, sans slender silk umbrella, and sans almost
anything'. Bare flesh could be seen in abundance at the seaside –
to the great alarm of many Englishmen. But their concern failed
to halt the rush to the sea.

Even where local authorities introduced bathing regulations,
as they did at Southport, visitors continued to complain of men
'shamefully exposing their person, to the great annoyance of
females'. These complaints, and the older criticisms of men
lurking near women's bathing machines, had long been a feature
of the hostility shown to seabathing, but the sheer volume of
seabathing by mid century made the problem all the more
obvious. Among female bathers who were suitably dressed for
the event, swimming seemed to induce unladylike behaviour,
which offended contemporaries as much as male nudity. The
Observer noted, in 1856, that on rough days

> the females do not venture beyond the surf, and lay themselves
> on their backs, waiting for the incoming waves, with their
> bathing dresses in a most dégagé style. The waves come, and
> in the majority of instances, not only cover the fair bathers, but
> literally carry their dresses up to their neck, so that, as far as
> decency is concerned, they might as well be without any
> dresses at all.

Not surprisingly, such sights were eagerly watched, and approved, by gentlemen with opera-glasses. Ladies too were
curious about the starker events on the men-only sections of the
beach – to the *Observer*'s great scandal: 'How is it that ladies
who are so delicate in London, should, when they arrive in
Reigate, throw off all pretensions to modesty and decency, as
they do their shawls and wrappers?'

Much of the explanation may lie in the numbers involved, for amongst large crowds of swimmers, when the 'water is black with bathers', men and women doubtless felt bold enough to behave as they could never do in private or in smaller groups. There is of course nothing particularly Victorian about this. But it may also be the case – and contemporary hostility suggests that it was – that the seaside offered the perfect occasion for dropping a number of prevailing conventions and restraints. To bathe in the sea offered visitors a refreshing contrast to everyday life; to be able to do so in the nude, or a state of relative undress, was to add the excitement of unconventional behaviour to the enjoyment of swimming.

Resorts posed dilemmas for morally sensitive Victorians. On the one hand, as more and more evidence came to light in the debate about the 'Condition of England', it was widely appreciated that recreation, leisure and, quite simply, breathing- and exercise-space for city-dwellers, were vital for their own and the national well-being. On the other hand, the powerful, religiously motivated restraints on private and public behaviour were challenged by new forms of leisure. Moreover, the seaside towns, with their increasingly varied entertainments, were peculiar cities where, in the season, tens of thousands rushed into a social vacuum. Trippers went to enjoy themselves, and generally left their more sober behaviour at home. Resorts were towns of an unusual kind and, while it is true that by mid century, England had become a predominantly urban society, contemporaries were at a loss to explain the whys and wherefores of mass behaviour at the seaside. To critical, unsympathetic eyes, visitors to the coast were regarded as not unlike lemmings; their inspiration for rushing to the sea was as mysterious as their behaviour on arrival. But still they came.

Beside the seaside, people found enjoyment in doing unusual things. A commentator noted in 1864: 'People at the seaside are for the most part intent upon doing nothing, and the object naturally is to do this in as great a variety of ways as possible . . . The only pursuit of men and women besides bathers, is looking at one another, and at the sea.' Those Englishmen whose energy demanded more than mere relaxation on holiday (perhaps because it was not consumed by hard and regular work) found the laziness of seaside life deplorable. 'A grown-up man cannot make mud pies, or build castles in the sand with wooden spades, and he is not as a rule, passionately devoted to donkey-riding. Yet, so far as I have been able to discover . . . these seem to be the main amusements for an intellectual public.' Children, on the other hand, seemed to find a natural habitat on the beach for their games, inventiveness and general enjoyment. But many Victorians, disdainful of popular pleasures which passed their comprehension, and unsympathetic to the fact that many people enjoyed doing absolutely nothing, found popular habits at the seaside dull and unimaginative.

Many people merely transferred to the resorts (and even to the beaches) the style of life they led at home. For the middle class, whose servants undertook the time-consuming task of looking after children, the beach in summer seemed to present a home from home. Dickens's Tuggs family found that on Ramsgate beach

> the ladies were employed in needlework, or watch-guard making or knitting, or reading novels; the gentlemen were reading newspapers and magazines, the children were digging holes in the sand with wooden spades, and collecting water therein; the nursemaids with their youngest charges in their arms, were running in after the waves, and then running back after them.

For a growing number of more adventurous Victorians, however, the seaside presented a marvellous opportunity to explore a growing science – the flora, fauna and geology of the coastline. Led by middle-class enthusiasts, anxious to teach themselves the details of marine biology and conchology, Victorians found on the coast living evidence of the wonders of nature – and a strong reproof to the more literal biblical interpretations of the earth's origins and structure. One man in particular, Philip Henry Gosse, was responsible for popularizing marine biology. From his home on the Devon coast, Gosse produced a string of influential and original books in which he 'displayed the wonders of life lying concealed within rock pools, among rich carpets of seaweed or to be dug from beneath the sand'. His books sold well to that prosperous middle-class readership which sought both the respectability of education and the pleasures of the seaside. In Gosse's books they were able to enjoy the two together.

As he became more famous, Gosse led conducted tours of the rocks and seashore, as his son later recalled:

> My father strides ahead in an immense wide-wake, loose black coat and trousers, and fisherman's boots, with a collecting basket in one hand, a staff or a prod in the other. Then follow gentlemen of every age, all seemingly spectacled and old to me, and many ladies in the balloon costume of 1855, with shawls falling to a point from beneath between their shoulders to the edge of their flounced petticoats, each wearing a mushroom hat with streamers.

Gosse's work triggered off a veritable stream of literature connected with marine biology; best remembered today, perhaps, is Charles Kingsley's *The Water Babies*. The by-products of this interest were enormous and manifold. Academic work proliferated; women took up the study with zest (and in the process had to replace their elaborate clothes with more functional clothing); domestic aquaria became fashionable, swiftly followed by those at London Zoo and Crystal Palace. So popular did the collecting of shells, fossils and fauna become, that, by late century, it was thought to have caused irreparable damage to the coastline's wildlife. Shells – and objects made from shell – became standard souvenirs of a seaside visit (they are now expensive Victorian artefacts).

The Victorian preoccupation with the natural face of the seashore was not disturbed by the publication in 1859 of Darwin's *Origin of Species* for, though there was a consequent howl of religious and scientific rage, a multitude of earlier scientific tracts had challenged both biblical and scientific orthodoxy about the origins of the earth. There was, however, an undoubted general excitement about the state of scientific knowledge, and this excitement, at a humble and popular level, was easily experienced by interested Victorians simply by paddling along the seashore in search of those primitive forms of creature which seemed so germane to the debate about the origins of life.

The twenty years between the Crystal Palace Exhibition and the passing of the Bank Holiday Act in 1871 had witnessed the firm entrenchment of the English seaside holiday as a prominent form of mass leisure both for middle- and working-class people. They did not of course enjoy the same kind of holiday, even when visiting the same resort. Working people tended to travel as day-trippers; their superiors went for longer, and went farther afield. The limitations of time and money imposed crucial distinctions between working- and middle-class holiday-makers. But both master and man were united in their flight to the coast. 'Our seaport towns have been turned inside out,' wrote *The Times* in 1860. 'So infallible and unchanging are the attractions of the ocean that it is enough for any place to stand on the shore.'

For worker and employer, artisan and merchant, the seashore offered an invigorating change from the unhealthy grime of Victorian cities (even though it is true that the resorts were themselves classic Victorian cities). For those able to afford it, a prolonged visit to the coast offered better health, but so many of those in need of extensive holidays were obliged to clamber back into their excursion train later that same day. And many, many more remained at home, tied by economic and domestic circumstances to an unbending routine of work or family life. Despite the increasing number of visitors to the coast, it seems unlikely that by 1871 they outnumbered those who had never seen the sea. Until times got better, and working hours de-creased, whole groups of working people were unlikely ever to catch a glimpse of the sea.

The quarter of a century which followed the establishment of the Bank Holiday witnessed a massive upsurge in seaside visits and the reasons take us back, once again, to the changing economic circumstances of the times. The years 1873–96, often called 'The Great Depression', saw an emergence of new areas of economic activity which has often been masked by the more troubled experiences of the older, heavier industries. The dominance of old industries was slowly being whittled down and, according to G. M. Young, 'capital, labour and intelligence were flowing away to light industry, distribution and sales-manship.' Retail and distributive trades expanded; in 1880, for example, there were 1500 multiple stores – by 1900, 11,645. Holiday resorts were among the beneficiaries of the rising consumer power which lay behind these changes, and perhaps the most striking feature of the resorts themselves in the last twenty-five years of the nineteenth century, was their own growth and expansion. Bournemouth expanded most remarkably: in 1841 Dr Granville found fewer than thirty houses there, twenty years later the population was still less than 2000; but after 1870, when the town acquired a rail link, the population rocketed, until by 1931 it stood at 116,000. There were similar upswings in population in the late century at Hastings, Southport, Eastbourne, Blackpool and Southend. Southport's population of 22,274 (in 4217 homes) in 1871 had risen to 49,908 (in 9896) by 1901. Brighton's population of 90,000 in 1871 grew to 107,000 in 1881 (though in part this was due to changing boundaries), and to 123,000 in 1901.

The growth of seaside towns in the late century was clearly related to the changing *nature* of the resorts. Within the seaside towns in the last twenty-five years of the century there was a massive growth in leisure facilities, much of it the work of energetic financiers and entrepreneurs. The piers continued to characterize the fun of the seaside and their construction continued unabated; of fifty-four in existence today, thirty-three were constructed in the years 1870–1910. Existing piers were extended, their facilities widened and a variety of elaborate architectural additions heaped upon the original structure. Often the stark functional iron-work and wooden walks were literally buried beneath an abundance of ornate façades. And, as the century advanced, the appendages to the piers began to diminish the appeal of the basic structure; the piers of 1890 were (at least to modern eyes) uglier than the piers of the 1860s. Popular taste, or rather the entrepreneurial view of what constituted popular taste, became more and more striking in seaside architecture.

The piers, and the traditional recreations to be found on the piers, were increasingly under pressure from new forms of entertainment created by a new breed of entrepreneur, anxious to tap the growing purchasing power of visitors. Theatres, music-halls, pleasure gardens, penny-in-the-slot machines, zoos and musical facilities of all kinds sprang up in the resorts. The case of Rhyl – within easy railway reach of the Lancashire towns and the Five Towns of the Potteries – offers an interesting case study. In 1876 the Winter Gardens were opened, offering an unusually varied range of recreations: theatre, zoo, bear-pit, seal pond and skating-rink. By 1902, when the Queen's Palace was opened, the facilities were even more exotic for, in addition to the zoo, there was a ballroom which catered for 2000 couples, an artificial underground Venice and imitation gondolas. And a similar pattern could be repeated for most of the popular holiday resorts in those years. But many of the leisure activities took place out of doors, originally on the beach or the promenade. Seaside towns everywhere had their own 'nigger minstrels' – that peculiar offshoot of Americana which became a distinctive feature of popular entertainment in England. Nigger minstrels and female impersonators were legion, throughout the music-halls and at the seaside; how strange that so racist and sexist a society as Victorian England should so idolize imitation blacks and make-believe women. At Rhyl the nigger minstrels were so popular that in 1890 they were sponsored by the municipality; four years later they had acquired a permanent 'pitch'.

The inspiration behind the nigger minstrels was the performance of one T. D. Rice, in 1836. Within thirty years minstrels were everywhere – as Mayhew discovered in his London survey – and as the resorts grew in popularity, so too did the minstrels, their success at the resorts and on the halls securing for them a peculiar prominence in Victorian and Edwardian entertainment. By the late century they were 'kings of the Beach, the Promenade and the Pier', and though they offered comedy, banter and audience participation, it was their music which stood out. With cornets, concertinas, but above all with the banjo, they provided simple musical treats for the visitors. Like the brass-bands – but quite unlike the music-hall – the nigger minstrels presented respectable, 'clean', family entertainment. The 'Uncle Bones' and 'Uncle Mack' sported by every minstrel group were firm favourites with the children, who flocked to see them; a fact which, above all others, explains the ease with which the nigger minstrels' popularity was perpetuated from one generation to another. The nigger minstrels remained among the most formative of seaside memories for generations of children.

But in the 1890s the minstrels faced a new and serious challenge to their dominance of seaside music, in the form of the pierrots, introduced from France in 1891. The man who introduced the pierrots, Clifford Essex, set out specifically to capture the rich field of popular seaside entertainment. More gentle, refined, carefully dressed – and sporting female singers – the pierrots were instantly and hugely successful. By the mid 1890s they, rather than the minstrels, had come to characterize beach music and entertainment. Like other entrepreneurs who created other forms of seaside fun, the man who launched the pierrots did so for commercial reasons. Pierrots – like artistes travelling the halls – soon fell under the sway of managers and agents. One Blackpool troupe of pierrots soon controlled fifteen others at various resorts; another at Scarborough was later able to control theatres there and at other resorts. Personal fortunes, as well as a new musical form, blossomed from the pierrot shows.

Pierrots and nigger minstrels, in their turn, became highly professional, falling under the orbital pull of theatrical agents, managers, music publishers, music-hall proprietors – and seaside landladies. Those landladies who specialized in catering for theatrical troupes – with their unusual hours and habits – gathered at the railway ticket-barriers on Sunday evenings to collect their clients, or to tout for custom among the less well-organized artistes arriving with no rooms booked. In their turn the uncommitted artistes would 'judge the assembled landladies at the ticket barrier by the whiteness of their aprons'.

There was clearly an abundance of money to be had at the seaside and the visitors spent it liberally; people whose lives were featured by frugality and industry seemed (perhaps for those same reasons) to become more spendthrift beside the sea. As more and more working people arrived at the resorts with spare cash, the entrepreneurs, who came to dominate the resorts' entertainments, gave them ample opportunity to spend it; the pain of leaving town with little or no money was blunted by the pleasures experienced. The apparent reckless spending of working people at the seaside, produced a spate of popular myths: that working people regarded their visits as a failure unless they returned penniless and, even more absurdly, the belief that Lancastrian textile workers threw away their spare cash on the way home. Such myths are of course (like many other superstitions) more revealing about those who believed and repeated them than they are about the objects of the story, and suggest the unusualness of large groups of working people spending money in the pursuit of pleasure. Individually, working people may only have had small amounts to spend on the seaside trip; collectively, however, it amounted to a considerable sum.

Nigger minstrels and pierrots were only the two most obvious examples of light musical entertainment easily and cheaply available throughout the summer season. German bands, brass-bands, military bands, light orchestras, wandering players, organists in the theatres, sing-songs of all kinds – all competed for the public's musical attention. The sound of music was never far away at the summer resort – so much so that many considered it to be a hindrance to a quiet holiday. Writing from Broadstairs, as early as 1847, Dickens noted, 'Unless it pours with rain I cannot write half an hour without the most ex-cruciating organs, fiddles, bells or glee-singers.' A similarly jaundiced visitor wrote in *Punch* in 1877 that at 9 a.m. he was 'regaled with music of a German band attempting to get through the overture to *Zampa* with a clarinet, a cornet, a trombone, all more or less beginners'. At 7 p.m. the visitors' enjoyment was completed by another musical offering: 'Town band dreadfully noisy and awfully out of tune.'

While the resorts offered a focus for such musical activity, it was only one dimension of a mass musical culture which, ranging from chapel and church choirs through choral societies, brass-, silver- and reed-bands, to singing and playing within the home, all added up to a rich and vibrant musical environment. By 1889, for example, there were an estimated 40,000 brass-bands across the country and so firmly entrenched had brass-band music become that, led by Elgar, 'serious' composers, who had previously ignored the genre, began to write specifically for the bands. The consequent critical reappraisal of brass-bands and their music led, in the late century, to a further rise in their popularity. Tens of thousands paid to listen; municipalities and financiers offered substantial prizes; the bands began to travel the world. The musical instruments were expensive, and to buy them (and to dress in the ornate uniforms) thousands of working men were offered a rudimentary form of hire-purchase. And the flowering of the brass-bands – like that of mass football

and the seaside towns – bears witness to the rising consumer
power both of the working men who sunk their spare cash into
the bands, and of the even larger numbers who travelled to
listen. Brass-band music was working-class music (though
fashioned in cooperation with their social betters), and it rang
out wherever working people gathered for rest or recreation.
At the seaside they gathered in unusually large, expectant
crowds, anxious to enjoy whatever the bands could offer. It is
worth recalling the words of the popular song which became a
signature tune for the seaside towns:

> Oh I do like to be beside the seaside
> Oh I do like to be beside the sea
> Oh I do like to stroll along the prom prom prom
> Where the brass band plays Tid–de–ly–om–pom–pom!

A great deal of seaside music was played out of doors and
was hence accessible to those who could not afford to pay the
small entrance fee to the bandstand or contribute when the 'hat'
was passed round. But there was a parallel evolution of indoor
entertainments. Theatres and music-halls – reflecting again the
changes in leisure to be found throughout the country – were,
like the pleasure beaches, bandstands and piers, built by ambitious individuals and groups keen to enhance their town's
attractions, and their own fortunes. In the last quarter of the
century, when 'the season' shifted to the coast, the thousands of
artistes who travelled the country from hall to hall switched
their attention to the resorts. The stars and the local artistes
specializing in appealing to holiday visitors of that particular
region, took up residence at the Winter Gardens, Queens and
Prince of Wales theatres dotted round the coast. Theatrical
impresarios and theatre owners, having established their
empires and fortunes in the cities, began to divert their interests
and investments to the resorts. That they were prepared to sink
considerable funds into lavish theatres, which could only be
filled for a fraction of the year, gives some indication of the
commercial lure of the resorts. In 1886, for instance, William
Broadhead, a Manchester builder, bought the Prince of Wales
Baths on Blackpool promenade and converted it into a theatre-
cum-swimming-pool. Using circus and aquatic artistes Broadhead developed a very successful theatre which embraced baths,

1. 'A Back-side and Front View of a Modern Fine Lady
or Swimming Venus at Ramsgate', 1805

2. George III's first bathe, Weymouth, 1789

3. 'Common objects at the sea-side – generally found upon the rocks at low water', a *Punch* cartoon of 1858

4. Blackpool pier, 1863

5. View of the North Pier, with the central beach, promenade, Tower and Big Wheel in the background, Blackpool, 1897

LANCASHIRE & YORKSHIRE
RAILWAY.

SEA BATHING
FOR THE
WORKING CLASSES.

ON AND AFTER SUNDAY MORNING NEXT,
and on each succeeding Sunday until further notice, with a view of
affording the benefit of

SEA
BATHING,
A Train will leave the following Stations for
FLEETWOOD AND BLACKPOOL.

FARES
THERE AND BACK THE SAME DAY.

	A.M.	Males.	Females & Children.
Leave Manchester at	6 0	3s. 0d.	1s. 6d.
„ Bolton at	6 20	2s. 6d.	1s. 3d.
„ Chorley at	7 10	2s. 0d.	1s. 6d.
„ Preston at	7 40	2s. 0d.	1s. 0d.

Arriving at Fleetwood at 9 a.m.

FROM SALFORD STATION.
MANCHESTER TO LIVERPOOL
FARES there and back same day.

	Males.	Females and Children.
At 7 a.m.	2s. 6d.	1s. 6d.

BURY TO LIVERPOOL, BLACKPOOL,
AND FLEETWOOD.
FARES there and back same day.

	Males.	Females and Children.
At 6 20 a.m.	2s. 6d.	1s. 6d.

Parties availing themselves of these trains will be enabled to
BATHE & REFRESH THEMSELVES
In ample time to attend a Place of Worship.

**These Trains will return punctually at 6 p.m., arriving
at Manchester about 8 and 9 p.m.**

The Tickets will take the Passengers to the above-named places for **ONE
FARE,** but for the purpose of preventing any unnecessary confusion or
BUSINESS ON THE SUNDAY, it is desirable that tickets be taken on
SATURDAY EVENING.

Bradshaw and Blacklock, Printers, 47, Brown-street, Manchester.

7. Eating oysters at the Star Inn, Blackpool

6. Railway advertisement of the 1840s

8. The beach near the North Pier with bathing machines
and Bailey's Hotel, Blackpool, 1890

9. Blackpool pleasure beach at the turn of the century

10. Camels on Blackpool beach, 1897

11. Blackpool donkeys, 1903

12. W. G. Bean's bicycle railway, Blackpool pleasure beach, 1896

13. The men's beach, Brighton, *c.* 1895

14. Volk's electric railway, Brighton, 1896–1901

15. Sand yachts were invented *c*. 1822 but they were prohibited on Southport beach after a collision with a bathing machine and not re-established until 1852

16. A band concert at the Municipal Gardens, Southport

17. Girls in their Sunday – best paddling by the Marine Drive, Southport

18. The first open-air bathing-pool in Southport was opened in 1914

19. Spooning at Yarmouth in the 1890s

20. Bathing machines at Brighton, 1891

21. The first 'Concert Party' at Weymouth, 1894.
'Concert Party' was the term used for seaside entertainment

22. Will Catlin's Pierrots at Scarborough, 1898.
They gave three shows a day 'weather and tide permitting' and five on Bank Holidays·

23. The Magnets at Barmouth, 1908.
They gave performances on a platform on the sands at 11 a.m. and 8 p.m.

24. The R.A.F. exercising on Blackpool beach, November, 1940

25. Rigby Road Coach Station, Blackpool, 1947

26. Beside the seaside, Blackpool, 1939

theatre and music-hall. The 1d. programme song-sheet enabled the customers to join in the singing in a show which lasted three hours, and which was staged three times each day. Seaside halls were used more intensively – if not extensively – than their counterparts in the inland towns and cities. Not surprisingly, William Broadhead owned ten theatres at his death; his family later added a further eight to the family empire.

The quality and role of entertainment in the music-hall have been endlessly discussed and analysed. But, whatever the judgement, there can be no denying the omnipresence, in the last twenty years of the century, of a musical culture spawned by the halls. In 1899 George Gamble in *The Halls* noted:

> From the music-hall come the melodies that fill the public mind; from the music-hall come the catch-words that fill the public mouth. But for the fecundity of the music-hall, how barren would be the land, how void the chit-chat of the drawing rooms, the parlours, the sculleries! . . . In what way, other than parrotising the latest witticism . . . would the Bank-holiday makers conceal their boredom, if there were no waltz-refrains? And how would the urban and suburban classes and masses beguile the tedium of slow hours, and find an excuse for pausing in their 'life-work', if there were no barrel organs to brinkerty-brankerty, crinkerty-crankerty, drinkerty-drankerty – and so on through a whole horrisonous alphabet of machine-made discord?

And nowhere was this musical cacophany more all-pervasive than beside the sea in the summer months.

By the turn of the century, seaside entertainments were characterized not simply by heavy capital investment, but by the harnessing of a number of technical innovations, which were similarly transforming leisure elsewhere. The availability of cheap electricity, for example, made many of the bigger seaside entertainments possible. Blackpool's Tower was opened in 1894 – a pale imitation of the Paris landmark; two years later it was joined by a big wheel, constructed from 1000 tons of steel (and inspired by the Earls Court Wheel of 1895). The new roller-coasters which whisked holiday-makers through painful twists and dives were similarly dependent on electricity. At Brighton, Volk's electric railway trundled visitors through the sea on a peculiar machine which looked like a cross between a pier and an elevated tram. Electric lighting itself was a seaside attraction, for the lengths of the seaside promenades and piers were, from the 1880s, provided with a ribbon of colourful lighting, enabling the visitors to stroll up and down the prom until late at night. Electric trolley-buses provided transport along the sea-front and some piers even added electric trains as an extra attraction. The 'pleasure beaches' which sprang up in the early years of the twentieth century – often in direct imitation of the gaudier North American versions – were monuments to cheap electric power and light. Rudimentary films, soon to oust magic-lantern slides, also began to appear at the seaside. In 1897, for instance, at Rhyl, a Mr Cheetham presented the town's first 'living picture' show, and in September of the following year the *Rhyl Journal* recorded: 'We understand that Mr Cheetham has during the past weeks been making a new camera to take animated photographs of 1000 feet at a time. He has arranged to take a picture of the Blackburn Rovers versus West Bromwich match at Blackburn on Saturday next.'

Most of the early films, however, came from across the Atlantic. America was well ahead of Britain in the technical perfection of new forms of leisure, and – as a more advanced and prosperous nation – was more commercially aware of the economic potential of mass leisure. Not surprisingly, the influence of American forms of leisure and entertainment swiftly penetrated the British market; American gadgets and ideas were soon adopted by enterprising seaside entrepreneurs and British music-hall stars were just as quickly seduced across to join the embryonic film industry.

The perfection of the modern bicycle and the consequent bicycle craze of the 1890s added yet another new feature to seaside life. Although they could be found in droves throughout the country, bikes were ideally suited for cheap and easy conveyance of visitors up and down the proms. At Yarmouth, in 1888, a visitor found the prom 'filled with pedestrians, wheel-carriages and tricycles, some of them fitted with basket chairs in front driven by cyclists sitting behind'. Bicycles and tricycles rapidly became a feature of the resorts, plying their trade along-side the horse-drawn carriages and trams; they were, in effect, an English prototype of the rickshaw man. Another innovation of the late century was the trade in holiday photographs. Today, holiday snaps are essential souvenirs of previous holidays. By the turn of the century cheap and quickly produced photographs enabled the visitor to return home with a visual record of his time by the sea. And even the machines which came to clutter the piers, with their 1d. views of 'what the butler saw', were evidence of the capital investment, consumer power and technical change at work at the seaside. For one penny the tripper could enter the world of the upper class through the eyes of the curious butler, peep into the future or even play make-believe games of football. In fact the penny-in-the-slot machines which rapidly dotted seaside piers and pavilions were devised almost entirely for the provision of entertainment; to provide sweets, postcards and saucy views. Only later did the wider commercial potential of self-service machines become apparent. But in late Victorian England, such machines – themselves a product of the Victorian iron age – came to the aid of those men anxious to find new ways of extracting cash from the seaside visitor.

These, and a host of other innovations, the cheap by-products of technology and enterprise, expanded the facilities of English recreational life. But it is, nonetheless, still the case, that this rapid expansion in leisure facilities was part function, part cause of a changing economic climate. Just as working people were being released from work in growing numbers, so too were whole sections of economic activity turning to the rewarding and diverse tasks of catering for mass leisure. Technical and social change dovetailed in the pursuit of pleasure and profit and, though the seaside towns were not the only towns to witness a remarkable growth in popularity in the last twenty years of the century, they nonetheless exemplified the fundamental changes in English society's attitude towards mass leisure.

Not all seaside entertainment was organized or commercialized. There was an array of informal amusements, which clamoured for the visitors' attention (and cash), mainly offered by individual or small-group entertainers who could scarcely scratch a living from the seaside crowds. Indeed, the sheer volume of street, beach and peripatetic entertainment was one of the key forces which persuaded local authorities to legislate, control and license local entertainments. As with the music-halls nationally, the simple weight of entertainment demanded strict supervision, in the best interests of both performers and customers. Even the donkeys were licensed.

Throughout the nineteenth century, donkeys had been, like the minstrels, perennial children's favourites. As a feature of seaside life, the donkeys on English beaches pre-dated the arrival of the holiday-makers *en masse*, emerging as a more sedate and inexpensive alternative to the horse-racing and riding which, early in the nineteenth century, had been commonplace on many beaches. By late century, however, the donkey rides were specifically identified with children.

Children of the poorer visitors to the resorts had little or no financial independence (despite the important economic role they often played within family life). It is noticeable, however, that there was an expanding seaside market for children's toys and playthings. The buckets and spades, which to this day accompany children at play on the summer sands, were available in the mid and late nineteenth century. So, too, were the fishing and shrimping nets and baskets, but all these fixtures of the English seaside seem, even at the turn of the century, to have been generally the property of the more prosperous children. Of all children's seaside treats, perhaps the most distinctive were the Punch and Judy shows which, like so many other areas of entertainment, were practised by father and son for generations. With their colourful, unchanging story – a gruesome mixture of brutality and horror – Punch and Judy starred at all the major resorts, and were only to fade away in the years after the Second World War. But perhaps *the* greatest attraction of the seaside remained the simplicity of enjoyment on the beach. Children of even the poorest visitors did not need any hardware to enjoy themselves; they could dig and burrow, build and re-build with their bare hands. Some fun was of course expensive; much of it, however, was quite free.

The beach offered fun for all, irrespective of social station, though, in fact, social differences were obvious between and within resorts. The style of clothing – and activity – on different beaches (or different parts of the beach) clearly shows the fissures of social class which followed the Victorian English right down to the water's edge. But, in enjoying the benefits and freedom of the beach, the English offered the illusion of a nation united in its seaside enjoyments.

In June 1872 the Rev. Kilvert visited New Brighton, where he found the sands

> covered with middle-class Liverpool folks and children out for a holiday, digging in the sand, riding on horses and donkeys, having their photographs taken, and enjoying themselves generally. Some of the lady and gentlemen riders upon the hired horses were pitiable objects, bumping up and down upon their saddles like flour sacks, and even requiring their horses to be led from them.

One of the most distinctive features of the trip to the seaside was the fact that it was enjoyed *en famille*. In an age when popular leisure was often divided by sexual and age differences, the English seemed united by the seaside because their visits were family affairs. Life on the beach was enjoyed by both adults and children – an unusual sight in Victorian England.

Despite the decline in medical support for salt-water treatment, swimming maintained its appeal for Victorians, and whenever English middle- and upper-class visitors stayed on the coast, they headed for the water, often before breakfast. But for the day-tripper, swimming was often both inconvenient and expensive. More and more beaches were segregated for swimming (thus separating families), bathing machines added to the seaside expenses, and the encroachment of local by-laws demanded bathing-costumes. Not surprisingly, paddling at the water's edge developed into a major ceremony of seaside visits. And with trousers rolled up and skirts hitched high, paddling was enjoyed by young and old, men and women. There were clearly many people who would have liked to take the plunge but who found the physical inconveniences of swimming from a beach a little daunting; consequently, in order to appeal to this group, and to improve their local amenities, from the 1860s onwards resorts began to construct swimming-baths. Frequently using sea water, the baths offered the swimmers a more comfortable form of recreation, combining the virtues of sea water with the physical comforts which more and more Victorians expected of life. Moreover, in the last quarter of the century, swimming, like other sports, came to be valued both in itself and as a means of encouraging physical fitness. The cult of swimming grew enormously (made possible not by the flight to the sea, but by the provision of municipal swimming-pools). Like football, swimming became a common subject in the schools and its popularity (helped by Captain Webb's cross-Channel swim in 1875) led to rapid changes in swimming attire. As women's wear became more practical, and the swimmer revealed more of her body, there emerged the concept of the bathing beauty – a far cry from the shrouded ladies who dotted the shoreline in the early century.

Even when the weather was unsuitable for bathing – or watching the bathers – the seaside visitors could enjoy a variety of entertainers, who all helped to produce a climate of excitement. The musicians, strolling-players, acrobats, hawkers, hurdy-gurdy men, ventriloquists and escapologists, the magicians, clowns – and even the rogue itinerant evangelists – all added to the carnival atmosphere of the resorts in summer. Visitors to Llandudno crowded the prom to see Signor Ferrari and his collection of performing birds; high divers (often taking the title 'Professor') plunged from the pier. And the tumult of a busy day would often end with a firework display. There was entertainment for all tastes. In September 1872 the Rev. Kilvert ended a day at Weston-super-Mare by going 'to the Assembly rooms to a lecture on craniology and phrenology and mesmerism. A table full of skulls was set out and the lecture was given by a Mr Hume. We had seen it advertised on the pier.' The popular resorts were, in season, colourful, noisy and crowded, offering a range of entertainments unobtainable in such density anywhere else. By the turn of the century, the seaside towns were monuments to pleasure, and visitors flocked to them in their millions.

The arrival of visitors by the trainload had enormous consequences for the resorts, some of which were transformed by the sheer numbers. Some resorts made determined efforts, through the tightly knit coteries of local landowners who sought to exclude popular excursionists, to maintain a more genteel social ambience in their towns. Other towns, however, sought to reconcile excursionists with the gentility which had prevailed earlier in the century. New Brighton tried to do both – and failed to achieve either. Southport did succeed in maintaining a dual personality: Lord Street had the elegance and style of an

old watering place but the beach and shoreline provided all the
fun of the fair for northern working-class visitors. Scarborough,
too, provided the best of both worlds. Polite society continued
to frequent the town but, increasingly, in competition with the
lower social orders.

It seemed to me [said William Miller] that Scarboro' was
a good deal frequented by clerks and others who got a week's
holiday, or care to spend as much as a week's holiday would
cost. There was an incessant racket of music or other din to
keep up which could afford no relief to wearied brains and
indeed gaiety was the order of the day.

This transformation was largely due to the large numbers
travelling to Scarborough by train from other parts of Yorkshire.

Even when a local council tried to resist the tide of visiting
humanity, it could do little to deter the informal structure of
entertainment which evolved to satisfy the pressing excursionists, and which caused so many public 'nuisances'. In the case of
Hastings,

the railways bring multitudes of day excursionists from London
and elsewhere which, added to the lodgers who come for a
week or more, make the beach, particularly at the Hastings
end, – the St Leonard's end is quieter – black with their
throng – the concourse often massing round exhibitors and
musicians of all kinds.

The story was the same at Brighton: 'On Sundays and holidays,
[it] is filled with crowds of excursionists. It may be said almost
to be a suburb of London.' At some resorts the main sight on a
summer's day was the crowd itself. William Miller thought
that at Yarmouth the chief sight of the summer season was the
immense crowd of excursionists which headed for the beach:
'There they lay in legions, engaged principally in watching the
bathers and young paddlers.' The scenes at Ramsgate exemplified the common face of the English seaside town so disliked by
fashionable visitors.

The shore was a mass of confused gatherings from the
great metropolis, tumbled upon it and packed as thickly as

they could sit or stand, as if all London had been thrown upon a cotton handkerchief – while in the midst and thick of this inpenetrable crowd some half-dozen small knots of musicians were sounding noisily and clanging, beating, and blowing their instruments within a few feet of each other, and only intent on increasing the din and collecting their half pence. Then here and there itinerant hawkers banded their wares, as if to illustrate all the cries of London.

By the turn of the century some resorts had developed a unique, often plebeian, character which seemed to cast aside the conventional inhibitions – a fact much bemoaned by the *Queen* in 1900:

> It cannot be denied that numbers of persons of the 'robustrious' temperament feel themselves exhilarated by all these accessions – niggers, musical performers of varying degrees of discord, overcrowded wagonettes and steam trips, pier entertainments, and the rest, which affect adversely those with finer nerves . . . Then there are the young ladies, perfectly decorous and well-behaved in London who give themselves up to *abandon* on piers and other public places which is astonishing.

Among the popular resorts, Southport, Scarborough, Hastings, Brighton and Ramsgate found their immediate historical roots in the old traditions of the watering place. Yet all were undoubtedly transformed – to various degrees – by the conjunction of rail travel and the ability of tens of thousands of working people to afford the excursion fares. Like it or not – and there was no real effective ban on plebeian travel from London and the industrial cities – residents, corporations, property-owners, or traditional long-stay visitors in the older resorts could do little to hold back the waves of lower-class day-trippers which cascaded on to the shoreline at weekends and throughout the summer season. Some resorts (Bournemouth being perhaps the best example) whose railway link came late, or which were too distant for effective day-trips, were able to maintain their social aloofness and preserve themselves for visitors of a better sort. From Bournemouth west into Devon and Cornwall this tended to be the pattern, and poorer visitors did not, in general, break through into that preserve of the wealthier and the middle-class sick and old, until the inter-war years. Nonetheless, the trains took more and more people away from the grime of the cities to the fun and fresh air of the coast. There, if only for a few hours, working people were able to emulate their social betters and hastily gulp the sea air, paddle in the sea and enjoy the panorama of seaside entertain-ments. But, in direct proportion to the rise of working-class seaside visits, the better-off sections of society fled – to un-disturbed parts of the same town, to remoter spots far from the crowds or, best of all, across the Channel to the delights of Europe and the Mediterranean. Such undreamed-of visits were to be a long time in coming the way of working people. In the meantime, however, Blackpool seemed no less appealing than Biarritz.

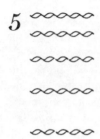

5   *Into a New Century*

∾∾∾∾∾ The accession of Edward VII symbolized more than a mere change of monarch, for the new king's obvious self-indulgence contrasted sharply with his mother's austere widow's style. Edward was keen to transform the tone of the English monarchy and he was, of course, well-qualified for the task, having spent an apprenticeship of some decades in the pursuit of pleasure. His was a well-known face at gambling-tables, watering places and landed estates throughout Europe; the rest of his corpulent person, equally familiar throughout the bedrooms of fashionable Europe. In the decades when millions of his subjects were slowly emerging from a morass of industrial and urban deprivation (though millions still remained trapped by it), Edward had devoted his full attention and considerable efforts to personal gratification. The irony remains that he was a popular man whose publicly known transgressions seemed to offend the prickly sensibilities of the English middle class, rather than those millions whose poverty stood in sharp contrast to Edward's financial recklessness. In retrospect he seems a well-qualified patron of a society which spent an increasing amount of time and money in search of leisure.

A change of monarch is, however, no more than a useful terminal point for historians, providing a helpful but often an artificial breathing space in the difficult task of imposing shape and order upon historical events. And while Edward lent his name to the years 1901–14 (though he died in 1910), many of the characteristic features of these years clearly owe their origins to fundamental forces at work late in the nineteenth century. The emergence of mass recreation and leisure, as we have seen, owed nothing to the monarchy (though royal and aristocratic fads had helped to shape the early popularity of particular resorts) or even to the work of government. And while it is true that working people, by the sheer weight of their numbers, had imposed a plebeian tone on certain resorts, the physical face of the resorts was the work of capitalists and entrepreneurs, local property-owners and financiers who invested in the towns' development. One basic consequence was that by the early century, even in towns like Blackpool, renowned as a working-class resort, the physical features were the work of the English entrepreneurial class. Like music-halls and football stadiums, the popular resorts of the early years of the twentieth century represented working-class culture emerging, not in isolation, but in a complex and often uncomfortable, harness with middle-class financial interests.

The resorts of Edwardian England were more popular than ever and, significantly, they found their way into more and more contemporary books and plays. Arnold Bennett's novel *The Card*, published in 1911, told the story of Denry Machin who travelled from the Potteries to Llandudno ('being more stylish than either Rhyl or Blackpool, and not dearer'):

> Denry had never seen the sea before. As, in his gayest clothes, he strolled along the esplanade or on the pier between those two girls in their gayest clothes, and mingled with the immense crowds of pleasure-seekers and money-spenders he was undoubtedly much impressed by the beauty and grandeur of the sea. But what impressed him far more . . . was the field for profitable commercial enterprise which a place like Llandudno presented.

A year after the publication of *The Card*, Stanley Houghton's play *Hindle Wakes* received popular acclaim on the London and provincial stage. Its story centred on a Lancashire mill-girl who had met her employer's son on a Bank Holiday trip to Blackpool and who subsequently spent a weekend with him at Llandudno. Yet the fictional seaside was no more daring or unusual than the summer reality.

The lure of the resorts grew stronger partly because there was a massive rise in the country's population, of which an increasing proportion were living in cities. Whereas in 1851, 50 per cent of the population were town-dwellers, by 1911 this had risen to 80 per cent. This fact, coupled to the sheer rise in population (which by 1911 stood at 40 million), meant that demographic pressure alone would accentuate existing social and economic demands. Seaside holidays became more popular quite simply because the population had greatly increased – irrespective of changes in economic fortunes. The seaside resorts mirrored the nationwide urban growth, as more and more people found a home on the coast. Between 1901 and 1914 the population of Blackpool grew from 47,000 to 61,000; of Southend from 29,000 to 63,000; of Bournemouth from 47,000 to 79,000 and of Brighton from 123,000 to 131,000. They, and others, had become major towns in their own right – but of course their populations swelled to even greater size in the summer season.

The main focus of the summer season remained the beach, but bathing habits were changing quite perceptibly. The old sexual segregation on the beaches began to break down and mixed bathing rapidly became acceptable. In part, this change was inspired by the mixed bathing to be found on French beaches – some of which were easily and cheaply reached by day-trips across the Channel. But mixed bathing was also made possible by the decline in nude bathing and while some (especially the gangs of young boys) continued to defy the authorities by swimming naked, the growing availability of cheap swimming-costumes was equally responsible. In 1901, Bexhill was among the first to sanction mixed bathing and soon other resorts began to advertise the existence of mixed-bathing facilities, which by 1914 were commonplace around the coast. In August of that year, *Punch* reported from the Isle of Wight that 'men, women and children have been swimming and splashing joyfully in a most mixed manner.'

Styles of swimming-costumes also changed; the older, cumbersome serge costumes giving way to much more revealing and more functional ladies' costumes which, when wet, clung revealingly to the body. Men's fashions similarly changed, and men could now be seen swimming on English beaches wearing swimming-trunks rather than the all-embracing costumes. France, again, seems to have been the inspiration behind these sartorial changes; but the acceptability of the new costumes was a function of changing English social attitudes and practice. It is difficult, however, to assess which social groups were able to afford the new costumes, though they seem to have been uncommon among the day-trippers. Whoever wore the costumes, it clearly was now easier and more acceptable to change on the beach. Thus, although bathing machines continued to dot the shoreline they were no longer essential, and large numbers of them were withdrawn (often to become allotment and garden sheds). In addition, cheap, lightweight materials were now available for easily constructed tents and awnings, so that beach changing-tents took the place of the more clumsy wooden machines. These same materials enabled the new holiday vogue of camping to establish itself, before the Great War. Camping had the virtue of being both cheap and apparently healthy, and a string of camp-sites sprang up around the English coast, catering primarily for young men. 'The young man with but a few shillings in his pocket', wrote the *Blackpool Magazine* in 1911, 'may spend a few happy days by the seaside or in the country, but young women are not quite so fortunate.' Thanks to the work of a dedicated band of pioneers, portable camping-equipment was perfected and the value of a few days under canvas was rapidly disseminated.

In the years immediately before the First World War the innovation which promised to revolutionize English social life, more than any other, was the arrival of the motor car. By 1908, for example, large numbers of Sunday trippers from London to near-by resorts were being carried by road, and not rail, though this may merely have reflected the peculiarities and difficulties of organizing anything other than a visit to church on an English Sunday. Car owners, however, were unlikely, for social reasons, to seek the dubious delights enjoyed by their inferiors, though it is true that the car was also revolutionizing the leisure of the upper classes, making possible the country weekend and extending the shooting-season. But the major impact of motor transport on mass leisure did not fully materialize until after the Great War. People able to afford a car fled from those areas and resorts now colonized by the lower classes, travelling instead to Europe – to Germany, Italy and the Riviera. It was consequently claimed that, 'Society ignored the English resorts', and while this was partly because of the widening horizons of people of means, and partly because continental resorts, notably on the

Riviera, were developing to cater for north Europeans, it nonetheless fits a pattern first established in the early years of the railways. Whenever the lower (and even the middle) reaches of society began to intrude into what had previously been the preserve of the upper class, the latter found reasons for going elsewhere. Some piously believed that holidays draw the English together:

And even if lower, middle and upper classes fail to mingle freely, they are, at least, brought closer together, and made better acquainted with each other's nature and character. In fact, the entire holiday movement tends towards the same increase of knowledge, the same better understandings, the same realisation of one another's virtues.

For the self-confident Edwardian bourgeoisie, the seaside resort offered a welcome break from the profitable routines of city life. But, for many middle-class gentlemen the commitment to a useful and industrious life was not arrested simply by visiting the seaside. Writing of her Edwardian childhood, Clare Leighton remembers that: 'Nobody in our household ever stopped working. Precisely the same pattern of life was led at the seaside as in St John's Wood . . . My mother had profound contempt for people who took holidays. She dismissed them as "having something common in their make-up".' The terminology is revealing: 'lazy' holidays were thought to belong to the lower orders. Her mother approved of two friends, 'for neither of them was off on such a plebeian thing as a holiday'. Clearly the lady was not condemning visits to the sea but denouncing holidays which involved wasting time, relaxing or merely enjoying oneself there. For the ordinary 'plebeian' visitor to the coast, the seaside involved a complete break from the routines and work of everyday life. Clare Leighton's family was different: 'Our family didn't go to . . . Lowestoft to take a holiday. We never took holidays. We went there so that we children should benefit in our health, and in order that our mother and father might go on working with additional vitality.'

Even the holiday needs of the middle-class visitors were catered for by those enterprising industries keen to tap the potential wealth of seaside visitors. Ladies – their children cared for by nannies – could fill their summer hours with volumes of stories published especially for holiday-makers. Cheap paperback *Seaside Stories*, packed with easily digestible love stories and mysteries, were available for a few pence. The fact that the publishers made special provision for this market is, like the manufacture of children's seaside toys, significant. Even the children of more prosperous holiday-makers were provided with cheap seaside reading. Yet those beautifully illustrated and socially self-conscious books of the Edwardian middle-class child gave no indication of the other social classes invading the coast at the same time. Their literature, like much of their real world, was, in fact, immune to the popular pressure from below.

Many Edwardian middle-class gentlemen packed their families off to the coast for the summer while they continued to work. Others, however, found it easy to conduct their business from the resorts. But the leisure they – and their wives – were able to enjoy was due, almost entirely, to the fact that they could afford to employ domestics for essential family chores. Osbert Lancaster, recalling his own Edwardian childhood, wrote: 'Each summer at the beginning of August I was sent with my nurse to an admirable boarding-house kept by an old governess of my father's at Littlehampton, where in due course I would be joined by my parents.' Whereas for poorer visitors to the seaside children were an ever-present care and worry, for the English middle and upper classes parenthood was delegated to the menials. And for the nannies, cooks, servants and others, the summer migration to the seaside involved merely a shift in location, with few compensations of extra leisure. Domestics – at 2 million still the largest occupational group in England in 1914 – were tied to their daily routines, which continued unabated at the seaside. Uniformed nannies – those foster parents of the English middle and upper classes – could be seen on the proms of English resorts wherever their employers spent their holidays.

Like the domestics, there were many working people who went to the coast not for relaxation but to find work. There were tens of thousands of summer workers in the resorts, in lodging-houses, hotels, transport and entertainments, whose collective efforts made the summer season possible. At the turn of the century, for example, 142 trains were needed every

Sunday in England and Wales, simply to move the multitude of theatrical troupes around the country. There is no way of knowing the number of temporary workers at the summer resorts but it was (and remains) considerable. However, for most working people the seaside was an alternative to, an escape from, work. Lazy holidays may have been denounced as 'plebeian' but therein lay their charm and virtue. Few commentators were as sympathetic as the Dean of Manchester who wrote in 1913 of the need for working people to relax completely on their holidays; and, on the whole, middle-class derision of seaside inactivity has formed a descant to working-class holidays in the twentieth century. When, in 1947, a researcher condemned the new vogue of holiday camps ('exploiting the indolence of people who want a holiday but who are too lazy to organise it for themselves'), he was only the latest in a long line of critics who failed to understand the basis of the popular holiday.

It is extremely difficult, however, to offer more than an imprecise guess about which groups of working people went to the seaside on the eve of the First World War. Not surprisingly, among the very poor a visit to the coast seems to have been an unattainable luxury. Remembering his own childhood in a Salford slum, Robert Roberts records: 'One scrimped and saved to get a new piece of oilcloth, a rag rug, the day at Southport, a pair of framed pictures.' Yet regular visits to the seaside among his poor neighbours were uncommon: 'Our top people paid annual visits to Blackpool, New Brighton and Southport and made sure that everyone knew, especially about their first ride in a motor car.' On the other hand, Booth's evidence from London in 1903, shows that day-trips, particularly on August Bank Holiday, were common even in the poorest districts. And other contemporary evidence suggests a similar picture. Writing, sarcastically, in 1909, C. F. G. Masterman suggested that the future 'millennium' might offer 'fourteen days of boisterous delight at Blackpool where now there are only seven'. It seems likely that only the better-off groups of working people could afford such an extended holiday. There were notable divides within working-class society; shades and nuances which marked off sub-groups from one another. On the one hand there existed 30 per cent of the population which both Booth and Rowntree had found to be on or below the breadline. On the other hand, however, were those in more comfortable circumstances, many of whom, according to T. O. Lloyd, 'had a vote (if male), would often be union members or skilled craftsmen working on their own account, or would aspire to some aspect of respectability if they chose to'.

But holiday trips to the coast were not restricted to this 'aristocracy of labour'. Poor children and young working people (many of whom, in those days of early school-leaving, were scarcely beyond adolescence) were often treated to free or subsidized excursions to the coast by churches, Sunday-schools or even factories. Yet this evidence seems scarcely compatible with the glimpses into Edwardian urban squalor afforded by the work of ranks of investigators: the work of Lord George Hamilton on the Poor Law Commission, C. F. G. Masterman, Mrs Pember Reeves in her book *Round about a Pound a Week* – these and many others painted an appalling picture of the extent and depths of poverty in Britain. The desperately poor formed a substantial part of the population; it was all they could do to keep body and soul together, and, for them, the luxuries of organized leisure or travel to the resorts must have remained mere daydreams.

Even among those workers thought to be rising in the world, conditions remained harsh. Looking back to his political campaigns in Oldham at the turn of the century, Winston Churchill recalled: 'There were many thousands of contented working-class homes where for more than a century things had been getting slowly and surely better. They were rising in the scale of prosperity, with woollen shawls over the girls' heads, wooden clogs on their feet, and bare-foot children.' These hardly seem to be the trappings of prosperity. And yet thousands of these same people trekked to Blackpool on day-trips, particularly at the annual Wakes holidays when the cotton mills closed down for the year's overhaul. It seems clear that in the early years of the twentieth century, urban poverty and rising expectations (of life and leisure) were not so much incompatible as uncomfortable bedmates.

Regular employment in the years before 1914 did not, in itself, guarantee enjoyment of the new, widespread leisure facilities. What was needed – apart from regular work – was the ability to save. Most industries guaranteed breaks from work, but holidays with pay were exceptional. In the early years of the century, however, unions took up the demand for paid holidays and some were able to secure concessions. Such holiday provision appeared in collective agreements in the railway services, the public utilities and the newspaper industries, providing workers with between three and twelve days off work. But these remained exceptional. Some paternal companies cut working hours more generously than they were obliged to do, either by factory legislation or by union agreement. In York in 1900, for example, where other factories were working fifty-four hours a week, Rowntree reduced their workers' load to forty-eight hours. Though regular paid holidays were rare, it was much more common to find individual companies providing holidays with pay as an incentive for good, steady work or punctuality. As early as 1884 a large chemical firm granted a week's paid holiday to those of its workers with fewer than ten unexcused absent days or shifts. In the last twenty years of the nineteenth century a number of individual firms began to grant paid holidays to their workers, and it was particularly common among municipalities and public services in London. By 1902 a prominent chemical company began to give two-week paid holidays, having learned the lesson, first established by the Factory Acts in the 1840s, that a rest from work was mutually beneficial to master and man. The company noted:

> It was always desired that a man should go away from home for his holiday, in order to get a thorough change. Yet it appeared that in a very few cases did he do so, and enquiries elicited the statement that he could not afford to go away and take the family, and that if he went away alone he left very little money for housekeeping.

Nonetheless, the scheme proved highly successful, and the number of beneficiaries eligible rose steadily from the original 42 per cent of the work-force in 1884.

A similar scheme was established by Lever Brothers, the soap manufacturers, who gave a week's paid holiday (between May and September) to all who joined the firm's holiday club. The money, deducted from the workers' wages, received interest of 1d. per 4s. deposited. Such incentives, with obvious gains for management as well as labour, were slowly adopted in a range of industries before the war. In March 1910, for example, Sir William Mather, head of the giant Manchester engineering firm Mather and Platt, established a fund of £10,000 in company shares, the dividend from which was to be distributed as holiday pay among their workers. Sir William wrote to his son:

> It has occurred to me that the annual holiday might be more thoroughly enjoyed as a means of healthy recreation out of town, if a fund existed, the income of which could be distributed amongst the work people at both Salford and Park Works to help them to meet the expenses ... I hope that by the aid of the fund it will be easier for wife and family to share in a husband's recreation during the summer holiday.

Again, there were conditions: the scheme applied to men over twenty-one and women over eighteen, and only if they had no more than two days' absenteeism over the year.

Work people rapidly accepted these schemes. At a major soap and chemical firm, one week's holiday with pay was introduced for those employed for more than fifteen months on 1 August. In 1900 57 per cent of the work-force qualified for the award; by 1912 it had risen to 94 per cent – a clear indication of the scheme's attractiveness for both labour and management. The idea caught on in trade union circles and, by 1911, the T.U.C. resolved to press for holidays with pay for all workers – a far cry from the earlier dogged resistance put up by certain union leaders to the idea of paid holidays. Nonetheless, the bulk of union activity before the First World War remained the basic drive for better wages and conditions – and holidays with pay were to remain, for the very great majority of working people, an unexpected bonus provided by paternally minded management.

For most working people there was only one way of providing for a holiday – and that was to save for it. Fortunately there was, from the early nineteenth century, a firm tradition of saving among working people. In Lancashire, for instance, where the clubs were needed for the unpaid break of the annual Wakes weeks, considerable funds were amassed over the year. In 1913, in fourteen large Lancashire towns, for example, a sum just short of 1 million pounds was saved by the local labour force.

The ability to enjoy a holiday clearly depended not simply on free time and spare money, but on the personal and family commitments of any particular worker. In this sense it is obvious that working people went through different holiday phases, or different levels of ability to afford a holiday. Unattached young men in regular employment were in a better position than older workmates, whose families absorbed their spare income. And for similar reasons, the children of large, poorer families could, in general, only enjoy a seaside break when it was provided by a benefactor. Once a man's children had grown up, providing he and his wife were healthy, it was possible for a working man and his wife to enjoy, again, the pleasures of earlier years. But old age, like large families, tended to put leisure and holidays beyond a person's reach – unless it could be financed by relatives. In the years before 1914 there is a deceptively uniform pattern, of more and more working people enjoying visits to the coast. But beneath it there lay a complexity of economic forces which determined the individual's ability or inability to enjoy a seaside break – or any other form of relatively costly leisure.

With the growth of the seaside towns and the complex service and entertainment industries to serve them, for tens of thousands of working people, the resorts were places of work rather than rest. Pliable, unorganized and cheap labour was vital for the success of the holiday industry – for the hotels, boarding-houses and theatres. And it was, and remains to this day, ironic that working people should be able to enjoy their break from work only by virtue of the exploited labour of others. The demand for labour, both skilled and unskilled, was enormous in the summer season. Indeed, it was possible for visitors to the resorts to pay for their holidays by working for a few hours each day. Tolerable pianists and singers could secure free accommodation in boarding-houses in return for a few hours' entertainment, while clerks and typists paid their way by organizing the hotel managers' books.

English resorts were at their apogee in the years before the Great War, and for many contemporaries memories of Edwardian seaside summers were to characterize fond recollections,

long after the war had transformed English society beyond re-
call. Osbert Lancaster noted:

> The unbutlinised Littlehampton of those days represented
> the English seaside at its best. Separated from the sea by the
> wide expanse of green, rows of bow-fronted Regency villas
> looked across the Channel; on the sands pierrots, nigger
> minstrels, and on Sundays Evangelical Missioners, provided
> simple entertainment for those who had temporarily ex-
> hausted the delights of digging, paddling and donkey rides.

But 1914 was to lead to the immediate disappearance of a
particular seaside group which had, for decades, regaled the
visitors´with their own brand of music. The 'German bands',
composed, according to Lancaster, of 'rather plump elderly
gentlemen with long hair and thick glasses clad rather im-
probably in tight-braided hussar uniforms', simply vanished
from the face of seaside England. The refrain of a popular tune
became significant:

> Has anyone seen a *Ger*man band
> *Ger*man band
> *Ger*man band
> I've looked everywhere both near and far,
> Near and far,
> *Ja*, Ja, Ja,
> But I miss my Fritz
> What plays twiddley-bits
> On the big trombone.

Of all the groups who found employment at the early-
twentieth-century seaside, one, in particular, has special
significance for the historical reconstruction of seaside life. Photographers in late Victorian and Edwardian England were able
to capture images of the nation at play – for the first time in
history – and their surviving material provides a source of
historical documentation which is rich and rewarding, and
which often concerns people who traditionally leave few traces
in the records.

Visual evidence of life at the seaside did not of course begin
with the camera, for the endlessly curious spectacle at the resorts

regularly attracted artists and cartoonists from the late eighteenth century onwards. By the late nineteenth century, however, the work of the painter and the sketcher was rapidly replaced by that of the photographers who flocked to the resorts in growing numbers. There was a commercial market for photographs just as there was for leisure, and survivals of the craze for capturing a holiday 'snap' can be found in millions of homes and, more important for the historian, they rest, often uncatalogued, in many seaside archives. If confirmation is needed of the colourful, teeming and varied appeal of the resorts, it can be found in the uniquely important collections of seaside photographs. Few aspects of seaside life escaped the attention of the photographers, and their visual evidence adds depth and perception to the historical interpretation of the period. More important still, the photographs herald the emergence of a new kind of historical evidence – visual evidence – to complement (and complicate) the modern historian's tools of the trade.

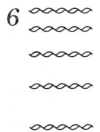

6   *Between the Wars*

The losses of the First World War left a profound scar on society, a scar which hid incurable personal and collective grief. Apart from the war-monuments erected across the country in their thousands, there were a multitude of reminders of the past four years. The economy, styles of dress, the role of women – to say nothing of the less obvious, intangible area of values and beliefs – all found themselves permanently altered by the experiences of the war. Long before hostilities ground to a halt, many people had come to the view that British society should be changed; it seemed absurd that the sacrifices and suffering in the war should result in a mere restitution of the pre-war *status quo*. Moreover, the determination to seek changes in British society was compounded, in certain circles, by the early enthusiasm for the revolution in Russia.

Through a complex change in attitudes, partly generated by the war, more and more people came to demand of life more than a mere marginal existence in a restricted social environment, but the post-war expectations were to be cruelly dashed. It was a sad irony that, as the nation slithered from its immediate post-war boom into the endemic depression of the 1920s and 1930s, many people who wanted a better life soon found themselves happy to cling to what they possessed.

From the mid years of the war, when industry and labour had been closely regulated and marshalled to feed the appetite of an all-consuming conflict, it had come to be appreciated that guaranteed rest and recreation were indispensable aspects of an efficient labour force. Looking forward to the era of post-war reconstruction, a Committee on Adult Education observed:

We believe that if a reasonable holiday without stoppage of pay were provided it would have a beneficent effect upon the national life . . . It may be that the question of holidays will, in the future, be the subject-matter of agreements between employers and employed, but in any case we think it important that the present custom among salaried workers with regard to payment during holidays should be extended to wage-earners.

The issue was taken up by the T.U.C. in a unanimous resolution, which affirmed that, 'the time has arrived for employers to make provision for and pay to all work people their wages at the recognised time rates of the districts for at least 10 working days holiday each year in addition to Bank Holidays.' Even without state intervention the number of wage-earners in receipt of paid holidays grew, because of the growth of the pre-war pattern of individual and collective agreements. By 1920, fifty-eight such agreements had been concluded, and by 1925 these figures had risen to 128. But the numbers of workers covered by such agreements declined, from 2 million in 1920 to $1\frac{1}{2}$ million in 1925, in direct consequence of the slump, though some $\frac{1}{2}$ million more received holidays with pay through private agreements. But even if we include this group it has been estimated that, by the mid 1920s, the number of workers receiving holidays with pay represented only 16–17 per cent of the wage-earning labour force.

By the bleak years of the mid 1920s, pressure for paid holidays looked ill-placed, and the main thrust of trade-union activity was simply to maintain employment and wage levels. The earlier, ambitious discussions about provisions for holidays seemed luxurious in the face of economic decline and rising unemployment. Holidays were, as in the previous century, very much dependent on prevailing economic prosperity, though there had been an undoubted shift in attitudes towards holidays which, increasingly, were considered to be a right. Those people who enjoyed them, however fleetingly, saw no reason to give up such enjoyable and refreshing breaks from work – even when work was hard to come by. But it was clear that an effective guarantee of holidays with pay – like the Bank Holidays in 1870 – could only be achieved by state intervention. Legislation was needed if working people were to be rescued from employers' regular, though perhaps legitimate, response, that economic hardship made holidays with pay impossible. To this end, a number of Private Members' Bills proposing the establishment of holidays with pay were introduced from 1929 onwards, but each attempt was deferred for various reasons. There was, nonetheless, obvious strong support for such legislation – but it was faced by a great deal of entrenched opposition and difficulty. Finally, in March 1937, a Parliamentary Committee was established to investigate the whole question of holidays with pay.

The committee, under the chairmanship of Lord Amulree, reported in April 1938, and its evidence and conclusions provide an invaluable synopsis of contemporary practice and attitudes, towards the wider field of holidays, in addition to sketching a useful history of the movement towards paid holidays since the early days of industrial change. It was clear that there was an acceleration of agreements providing for paid holidays – even as the committee sat – and that the practice was common in the distributive trades and in certain regions, 'such as the Wakes in Lancashire, the Bowlingtide holidays in the Woollen Industry in Yorkshire, and the Fair holidays in Glasgow'. Cotton employers interpreted the Wakes holidays as evidence that the workers did not need holidays with pay: 'The fact that most of the operatives in the Lancashire textile towns succeeded in going away to the holiday resorts and elsewhere during the customary yearly week of the summer holidays indicated that they were able to save sufficient from their weekly wages to meet this recurrent expense.' Nonetheless some $10\frac{3}{4}$ million working people did not receive paid holidays and, among those giving evidence to the committee, there was, as might be expected, dogged resistance to holidays with pay from groups of employers and manufacturers. Yet the overwhelming drift of the evidence was the belief that holidays were desirable and beneficial. The committee agreed: 'It cannot, in our view, be denied that an annual holiday contributes in a considerable measure to workpeople's happiness, health and efficiency, and we feel that the extension of the taking of consecutive days of holiday annually by workpeople would be of benefit to the community.'

One interesting argument in favour of paid holidays was the

feeling that it would remove 'the unfortunate distinction in this matter between workers engaged directly in production and "black-coated workers" which had no logical basis and was socially undesirable'. Perhaps in reaction to this distinction, and as a result of the general tide flowing towards holidays with pay, the evidence suggests that more and more working people regarded a paid holiday as their rightful lot. And for substantial numbers a holiday was synonymous with a visit to the seaside. Were legislation introduced, of the 11 million catered for, many would 'undoubtedly wish to make use of the facility to go away to the holiday resorts'. One witness after another made it clear that a working-class holiday meant a seaside holiday – to 'the places which are popular with working-class people, such as, in the north, Blackpool, and in the south, Margate and Brighton and similar places'.

Sir Walter Citrine of the T.U.C. argued strongly that 'workmen were not able or did not conceive of going for a week or a fortnight to the seaside in pre-war days.' A year later, a delegate to a conference on workers' holidays remarked:

> Our employees have had holidays with pay for over 30 years. At first they would either get another job for a week or live at home and go away for day trips; now practically all of them go away to the sea, to camp, to the Continent, or on cruises or coach tours.

Yet, as we have seen, hundreds of thousands of working people had indeed been deposited by the sea in the decades between the coming of the railways and the First World War. What had changed since then, however, was that large numbers of working people were able to spend longer by the sea. Whereas before 1914 the working-class seaside visitors had tended to be trippers, by the late 1930s they tended to stay for a week or more. And it was this pattern – itself a function of economic change – which was to remain a feature of working-class holidays until the 1960s. The spread of holidays – and of more extensive and expensive holidays – was more noticeable, of course, further up the social ladder, but in 1938 witness after witness spoke of the great untapped potential for more extensive holidays among working people.

Holiday-making expanded dramatically between the wars –

long before the holidays-with-pay legislation was introduced (and which in any case had not been fully operative before the dislocation of 1939). In 1935 *The Survey of London Life and Labour* noted that: 'An annual summer holiday is today taken for granted by a very large and increasing number of Londoners.' Various other sources confirm that this pattern was nationwide. The number of holidays organized by the Workers' Travel Association (an organization second only in size to Thomas Cook) is significant. Beginning in 1922 with 700 bookings, the business grew by leaps and bounds, registering the following increases: 1922–3, 185 per cent; 1923–4, 68 per cent; 1924–5, 79 per cent. Although the increase in holiday booking was maintained until 1931, the depression inevitably produced a drop, but from 1933 onwards the W.T.A. holiday trade once more perked up; it increased 30 per cent in 1936 and 40 per cent the following year. Ironically, there was no significant upsurge in holidays following the legislation of 1938. It seems that many of the people so recently 'enfranchised', could not make use of the paid break to take a real holiday. Ernest Bevin, the rock of the labour movement in the 1930s, was predictably confident that working people knew how to cope with paid holidays: 'Holidays mean more to people than being organised in the mass. The idea of a holiday is a breaking away from organisation and the cramping of the individual initiative. Give them the money and they know what to do with it.' In a sense this was clearly true – and it would be hard to claim that a paid holiday was wasted even when spent at home. But, despite Bevin's assertion, the holiday industries, from the railway companies through to the entertainers at the resorts, were geared to dealing with people *en masse* and had become highly efficient and organized at attracting and coping with armies of working people from the cities.

The mass entertainment industry continued to expand and to adapt itself in the inter-war years. Between 1931 and 1939, for instance, it increased by approximately 49 per cent – a greater rate of growth than any other industry – and while most of the growth was accounted for by the major changes in post-1918 entertainment (cinema, radio and dancing), the seaside resorts, as we shall see, were among the first to harness new entertainments to the never-ending task of making their towns even more attractive to visitors. The resorts launched expensive advertising campaigns – best remembered in some classic posters of the inter-war years – to seduce visitors to their towns. But, nonetheless, as holidays became ever more widespread, one factor remained constant. People tended to visit those resorts already visited by trusted friends. In choosing a resort – or holiday accommodation – working people were persuaded overwhelmingly by personal recommendation. Moreover, they knew that the well-established resorts, which exerted such gravitational pull within their own region, could cater for all their varied tastes and needs. There was, quite literally, something for everyone, and while it is true that not everyone was able to travel to the coast, a growing army did.

But the deciding factor remained finance, and for those with marginal incomes not even holidays with pay could guarantee a holiday away from home. In June 1939, the *News Chronicle* carried out a survey which showed that of those earning £4 a week or more, nine out of ten could afford a week away from home, but of those earning less than £4, only one third could afford such a treat. It was clear that the granting of holiday pay would not, in itself, make holidays for all possible. Even with paid holidays, the prospects of a summer break continued to depend on a man's level of regular earnings, and while it may be true that, in general, there was a slight improvement in living standards for a majority of people, the variations were very great. The Ministry of Labour figures for 1935, for example, showed that the average wage of 70s. per week included some groups earning 80s. and over, and others less than 50s.

Time and again, social surveys told the story of the other England – that strata of perhaps one third of the population, dominated by the old, sick, unemployed, and those with large families, who received less than was sufficient for a decent life. And yet we ought not to imagine that even among the poor, the resorts were utterly out of reach. Many of the old had been to the coast in younger days; charitable organizations traditionally arranged visits to the seaside for needy children. In the case of London, approximately one half of the city's school children enjoyed an annual holiday away from home and, though many were catered for by charitable trusts, two thirds were taken by friends or relatives. The day-trip continued to offer the best prospect for many working-class Londoners, as the 1935 survey of London labour showed: 'A large proportion, perhaps the majority, of London working-class families are still unable to reach this very modest standard [of a week's holiday] and have to be content with day outings on Bank Holidays or Sundays.' It is undoubtedly true, that even on the eve of the Second World War, the level of earnings required to sustain a full week's holiday away from home precluded substantial groups of working people. Increasing numbers of working people were indeed staying at the seaside, and more making day-trips; but substantial numbers were left behind.

The Amulree Report of 1938 pointed out that certain regions had powerful local customs of holiday-making which involved regular patterns of savings based on the workplace, the pub, peripatetic 'club man' and even the corner shop. And, wage levels apart, it was the existence of viable savings schemes which made many working-class holidays possible. A number of companies had, as part of their own schemes for holidays with pay, established savings-schemes. For example, of the 4500 employees at Lever Brothers' factories at Port Sunlight in 1938, 90 per cent contributed to the 'holiday club'. Paying in multiples of 6d., the average savings in the previous twelve months had been 7 guineas; that is, 3s. per week. And to this, the firm would add the interest over the past year, provided the sum were kept in the fund until the holiday itself. At the Dunlop factory, 40 per cent of the work-force belonged to the holiday club, making average savings of 50s.

One of the great virtues of such holiday savings-schemes was that, by deducting money direct from wages, it avoided the danger that the money might not reach the bank, though for many employees, these clubs acted as banks. One Lancashire worker noted: 'The Mill Club – as I well know – represents the easiest, handiest, and above all the surest way of saving money.' For many working people, banks were often far away, and opening hours were inconvenient. As with so many features of working-class society, life was clearly circumscribed and shaped by the work-place, the hours and conditions of work.

In the 1930s, the cost of taking a week's holiday was clearly high – relative to wages. Looking at the advertisements in *Dalton's Weekly House and Apartment Advertiser* in June 1934 (for Brighton, Southend, Clacton, Ramsgate and Hastings), investigators calculated an average holiday cost 35s. for full-board, rising to 42s. at the height of the season. This meant that a man with a wife and two children paid £6 6s. in July and August. When travel expenses, spending money and residual costs at home were added, the total cost of the holiday would certainly rise to £10. Four years later, in the summer of 1938, another investigator calculated that a man with a wife and two children needed between £5 and £8 for board and lodging, with bed and breakfast costing 25s. to 30s. per head. It was clearly cheaper (at perhaps £1) simply to rent a room, but self-catering holidays could hardly have been attractive to mothers in search of rest. And, in addition to these basic costs, the holiday-maker had to provide the cost of travel. Journeys from London to the south-coast resorts cost between 5s. and 13s., though it was noticeably cheaper to travel to the Lancashire coast from the textile towns. And all these costs exclude the unavoidable expenses of entertainments, which the resorts dangled so temptingly before parents and children.

Whatever the cost, there was, by the late 1930s, a rising urge for holidays, to the extent that some 15 million people spent at least one week's holiday away from home – that is, about one in three of the population. Traditionally, of course, the movement to the coast had been largely a function of railway development, and while it is true that the railway companies still carried the great bulk of seaside visitors, their virtual monopoly on holiday – and other – transport had been slowly eroded since the Great War by the massive advance of road transport. In 1901 there were merely 32,000 cars on British roads; by 1919 it had grown to 109,000; to 1 million by 1930 and 2 million in 1939. But it was the development of motor coach and bus transport which began to eat into railway transport to the coast. It is difficult to exaggerate the impact which road transport made on British life in the inter-war years. Within the cities, buses gradually took over from the trams; buses and coaches then pushed out, offering services between cities and, more importantly, linking previously isolated suburbs to the major urban areas. And in remote rural communities, the new bus services made it possible for areas which had been isolated – even from railway connections – to be drawn into their regional, economic and social network. And the consequences upon social and economic life, mobility and the movement of population were truly incalculable. (Ironically, a hint of these effects can currently be felt by examining the newly imposed isolation of rural communities recently cut off from bus services.)

It is, nonetheless, true that the railway trade to the coast continued to boom, and pressure on the railways in the summer season produced serious congestion throughout the 1930s. But the railways lacked the flexibility of the motor coach, which could not only open up new vistas for the tourists, but even pick them up at their own street corner. In the early days of motor coach development it was the holiday market to the coast which first attracted the enterprising coach operators. There was, clearly, a growing number of people anxious and able to travel to the coast, and there was a remarkable increase in the number of seats – on both coach and rail. The result was fierce competition between the road and rail companies, producing a dramatic fall in excursion prices. In 1930, for instance, one coach firm slashed the price of a trip to Blackpool from the West Riding from 7s. to 2s 6d., but this was largely a gesture in the commercial war for the lucrative market. Indeed, some idea of the commercial attachment which the railways had to the resorts can be gauged by their dogged resistance to the licensing of coach travel to the coast. And there was also fierce competition between coach companies for the licences between the cities and the coastal towns. So rapidly did coach travel expand, that some resorts which had not traditionally attracted large numbers of railway excursionists found themselves inundated with coach trippers.

Photographs of the inter-war resorts clearly show the impact made by motor coaches on the face of the towns. In the summer season, the promenades and streets of the resorts were lined and blocked by thousands of coaches and cars, forcing on the municipalities a particularly acute form of the general and growing problem of parking and traffic flow. Seaside authorities were forced to spend money simply to cope with the advent of motorized transport – a complete change of fortune from the days of the arrival of the railways in the previous century. But the motor coaches ('charas' to millions of people) brought more than mere congestion and extra people. They produced their own style of travel and their own holiday memories. Often filled with local people – a club, a street or church – frequently stopping at cafés and pubs, the chara trip became a distinctively working-class holiday itself, carrying large numbers of people to the coast – or country – and yet keeping them securely among friends and neighbours. There is something particularly cohesive about trips in a motor coach which is absent in a train and, for succeeding generations of working people and their children, the chara trip – captured by Richard Hoggart in *Uses of Literacy* – remains a formative experience and memory. Coach trips evolved their own games, their songs, their customs; the first child to catch sight of the sea – or Blackpool Tower – would win a sweet or chocolate. And the trip would inevitably end with the 'whip round' for the hard-working driver. The chara trip was collective travel on a small scale, whereby a group of local people could remain on familiar territory even when travelling miles from home. And it was, and remains, very noticeable that many working people, released from work for the same periods, often travelled to the resorts with relatives, workmates or neighbours. When visiting an unknown resort, familiar faces made it easier to cope with a new environment. The motor coach reinforced this sense of – and need for – collective identity among people whose lives were so measured out in collective terms. From the routines of the street, through to the more regimented details of the factory, working people found much of their identity and strength in the facts of collective life, and the emergence of modern seaside holidays was consistent with this experience. Relatives and friends of Robert Roberts took to the roads in the years after the First World War, as he recalled in his book *A Ragged Schooling*:

> Wealthier members of the proletariat, in their week's un-paid annual holidays, took *en masse* to motor char-à-banc tours round Britain. Middle- and upper-class people, resident in posh hotels and spas and along the south coast, were startled, then amazed to see horny-handed sons of toil and their spouses sitting, diffidently it is true, but sitting in the lounges and dining-rooms of places they had previously considered their own preserve. 'How in the world do they *do*

it, my dear?' 'Well, some of them did very nicely out of the war, you know – munitions.'

The effect on Roberts's mother was unsettling: 'A holiday glimpse of the paradisal south had strengthened mother's longing to be off anywhere out of the slums of Salford.'

Holidays and seaside visits had become established before 1914 but there was no doubt that motor transport both extended the nature and limits of holiday-making, and helped to reinforce the belief that holidays were as natural to a working life as a fair wage. Motor-coach travel helped the further democratization of the English holiday, as the Industrial Welfare Society commented in 1938: 'With the coming of motor buses, cheap cars and cycles there has been an enormous extension and cheapening of travel facilities, and this has led to widespread changes in social habits, so that holidays are now part of the standard of living aimed at by nearly everyone.' Commentators frequently returned to the powerful working-class commitment to holidays; 'an increasing factor in working-class life', according to Sir Walter Citrine. And, while it is true that more exotic – and far-flung – holidays were enjoyed by the middle and upper classes, the great expansion of domestic holidays took place among working people.

So great had the physical pressure of holiday and travel facilities become by the late 1930s, that the timing of holidays became a seriously debated problem. Holidays were largely concentrated in July and August, a fact 'determined by custom more than by its inherent attractiveness', and the August holiday congestion was worsened by the holidays-with-pay legislation. Employers and unions were generally agreed that some form of staggering was needed: 'Our aim is not to adapt tastes to the convenience of the "holiday industry" but to make it possible for the industry to meet the enormous increase in demand without sacrifice in quality or variety.' So great had the pressure of millions of people heading for the coast become, that some felt it questionable 'whether this can be handled adequately by voluntary means'.

The railway companies bore the full brunt of the problem. Figures suggested that in the decade between the late 1920s and 1930s holiday traffic on the railways had tripled. Furthermore, its greatest density was concentrated in a three-week period from July to August, and it was even more acute at the weekends of those weeks. 'The problem', said a railway official, 'is largely a Saturday one', and it was felt that, 'we have almost reached the breaking point on one or two Saturdays.' Nor was this mass of people evenly spread between resorts, for, 'everyone wants to concentrate on a limited number of seaside resorts and there is little encouragement to holiday makers to spread over the country and go to other places.'

The threat posed by holidays with pay, that the holiday market would double at a stroke, appalled all those involved in transport and the resorts' industries; it would have produced an even more alarming and uncontrollable phenomenon than the first August Bank Holiday legislation of seventy years before. And such a possibility highlighted the unplanned and, in many respects, unimagined consequences which could flow from a much-needed piece of reforming legislation. In granting a further concession of social justice, Parliament might actually inflict a previously unknown degree of social dislocation. In the event the expected deluge did not materialize – and the outbreak of war put the whole problem into cold storage. But all interested parties had legitimate cause for concern about the prospects of mass holiday-making.

Railway companies encouraged an 'Early Holiday Movement'; others organized a 'Spread-Over Holidays Campaign'. But the main problems were the ingrained routines and habits of particular regions and cities, and any change in the timing of holidays would have involved complicated negotiations with industry, unions and local school-authorities. On the eve of war it was only the fact that not all workers recently entitled to paid holidays, took their breaks at the seaside, which enabled the holiday industries to cope at all. Some gloomily predicted that 'neither commercial enterprise nor voluntary organisations could cope with it within the next four or five years'. But the war intervened and it was to be some years after that war before English society slowly readjusted to the social consequences of mass holidays.

The holidays-with-pay legislation which followed the Amulree Report of 1938 was largely a legislative consequence of the growth of holidays, and it could be argued that the legislation was a belated, parliamentary recognition of the expansion of holiday-making. The revolution in holidays was not restricted to the resorts, though they clearly bore its greatest weight – and reaped its richest dividends. Other, newer types of holiday had established a large following. After the First World War, Youth Hostelling developed into a major recreation, as had camping, and a number of camp-sites sprang up around the coast and in the country. But perhaps the most distinctive innovation in British holidaymaking was the holiday camp, which, though established in the 1930s, did not reach its peak of popularity until the 1950s. The first camp, established in 1924, was founded by the Civil Service Clerical Association, at Corton near Lowestoft, and many of the early camps were established by companies or staff associations for their own members. Holiday camps were of course to be personified by Billy Butlin, and yet he did not open his first commercial camp – at Skegness – until 1937, by which time there were more than a hundred camps able to accommodate ½ million holiday-makers.

Camping, in one form or another, had become a major industry and in 1939 some 1½ million holiday-makers took their holidays in camps or under canvas. Lever Brothers, who had long provided holidays with pay and works' savings-schemes also had a holiday camp close to the works on the coast. The austere, army-like regime at their camp did not blunt its appeal among married workers (though the younger ones, who were more independent, tended to go further afield). The Y.M.C.A. also experienced a boom in holidays, largely because of their provision of cheap family-holidays and it seemed apparent on all sides that there was a need for family-holiday facilities. But some also believed that all-inclusive holidays, particularly in camps with firm routines, were especially suited to the needs of working people. A gentleman from the London Co-operative Society said: 'The people now for the first time getting holidays with pay were used to a routine job and thus recreation was of the organised kind. More camps were necessary where amusements were provided all the time.'

The main difficulty facing all those organizations anxious to cater for the new working-class holiday-maker was to keep inclusive costs within the spending power of low-income groups. But the very construction of such camps involved capital outlay which made it difficult to provide cheap holidays. The Workers' Travel Association, founded in 1921 specifically to reduce the cost of working-class holidays, found its clientele demanding better (and therefore more expensive) facilities: 'The demand for better accommodation increased until now hot and cold water was necessary in the bedroom of the simplest guest-house.' And here – as elsewhere – their camps registered a positive demand for *family* holidays. Local authorities, too, were keen to build holiday camps, and yet they, like other organizations, found it possible to keep their charges low only if they did not include the capital costs. By 1938, the commercial rate in a holiday camp was 45s. per adult, and it was scarcely surprising that the bulk of the clientele appeared 'to be the clerical type'. On the eve of the war, and for some years afterwards, holiday campers were drawn very largely from 'smaller-salaried people', and there seemed no way of breaking into the potential working-class market, short of a massive rise in working-class consumer power. There was, nonetheless, a proliferation of holiday camps in the 1930s, and among the most peculiar were those catering for the middle-class intelligentsia anxious to pursue their intellectual interests under the austere circumstances of camp life. Today, this unusual mixture of intellectual single-mindedness and physical endurance can best be seen at Open University summer schools.

The camping and holiday-camp cult of the 1930s was, unpleasant as it seems, given a fillip by the apparent success of Nazi ideals – embodied in their camping and outdoor programmes – and was helped by the prevailing sense that outdoor life was one route to national well-being. Happily, the fascist holiday-cult in England was never more serious than a gathering of Mosley's Blackshirts at Bognor Regis.

Despite the expansion of these new forms of holidays – which, in any case, failed to make major inroads among working people – it was in the area of the more traditional seaside holiday that the greatest growth took place. And here, as in the case of transport, the problem of holiday congestion was particularly bad. Inevitably, at the peak of the summer season, prices for accommodation rose. Working people were limited in their choice of accommodation, primarily by finance: 'It is impossible to say what type of holiday people really want when they cannot afford to want anything but the cheapest', but also by the way they learned of accommodation. 86 per cent of holiday-makers found their lodging through recommendation, 12 per cent through advertisements, and a mere 2 per cent through travel bureaux. It was not surprising, then, that there were recurring patterns to working-class holidays, for people tended to take their holidays at the same time, travelled in locally based groups, stayed at well-proven boarding-houses and enjoyed familiar entertainments – all within the same approximate financial limits shared by friends and neighbours.

There was a firm belief, in the late 1930s, that holiday-makers enjoyed being part of a massive crowd – and such numbers seemed to suit the resorts: 'Landladies like a late Whitsun and crowds all the way; visitors like crowds, for they find the place more lively, holiday resorts like crowds because they can have more bands, illuminations and sideshows.' And yet the crowds which brought such commercial prosperity also brought the resorts to breaking point by the time of the Second World War. To cope with the millions of visitors the resorts embarked on massive investment in hotel- and house-building. By 1933 the total investment was worth £200–£300 million (some £10 million of which was held by railway companies). Between the wars, the seaside municipalities made enormous investments in their towns, both to cope with the growing numbers and to enhance the towns' attractions. In an era when other areas of social and industrial development flagged, the seaside towns were able to pour money into concrete and bricks. Blackpool exemplified the process, spending £1½ million on the promenade and gardens along the front, £100,000 on an open-air pool, £1¼ million on a park, a similar amount on the Winter Gardens, and £300,000 on an indoor pool. And all this in addition to other non-recreational investments. Moreover, the plans for further programmes were only curtailed by the overriding need to keep the rates down to 7s 6d. (a level which would delight and relieve present-day residents). This pattern could be traced, time and again, at resorts throughout the country. Indeed, it was estimated that the resorts spent £3–£4 million a year on improving their sea-front facilities, and the increasing exploitation of the English coastline began to alarm architects and urban-planners. The resorts threatened, by their very popularity, to destroy the natural attractions which had created them.

There was a consequent growth in the service industries, based on hotels, boarding-houses and clubs; a growth which can be gauged by the dramatic rise in the number of people they employed. In 1923 the industry employed 233,437; by 1930 it had grown to 311,000, to become the sixth-ranking industry in the country. Indeed, the rate of growth in the catering industry in the years between the war and the early 1930s was higher than in any other industry.

The nature and the pattern of accommodation available at the resorts was markedly different from one town to another. Blackpool, which in 1931 was considerably smaller than Brighton, had three times as many lodging- and boarding-houses, but Brighton had almost three times as many hotels. And similar differences existed between other towns – differences which tell us a great deal about the distinctions between resorts' populations, about their residents, the structure of local service industries, and the financial well-being of both residents and visitors. Blackpool, quite simply, attracted more visitors from the lower-income groups.

Understandably, the resorts' industries generated unusual employment patterns. Whereas the 1931 census showed a national average of 34·5 per cent of females over fourteen employed in personal service, the figures were much higher in the resorts; Blackpool had 55·5 per cent, Bournemouth 61·5 per cent, Brighton 52·5 per cent and the highest, Hove, 63·5 per cent. The patterns were equally unusual among men, where the national average of 3·54 per cent compared to 10·4 per cent in Blackpool, 9·5 per cent in Bournemouth and 8·6 per cent in Brighton. The 1931 census of retired people showed similar distortions of the national averages in the resorts; a national average of 5·5 per cent compared with 8·6 per cent at Blackpool, 10·8 per cent at Bournemouth and 6·9 per cent at Brighton. Resorts became obvious retirement centres for the more prosperous elderly in the region. The tendency was first in evidence in the previous century, but after the First World War this pattern was even more pronounced; Peacehaven in Sussex was developed specifically as a retirement town. The resorts themselves maintained their highly urban nature, first acquired in their nineteenth-century boom days. Nine of them in 1931 were classed among the country's 105 towns with populations over 50,000 while four – Brighton, Bournemouth, Blackpool and Southend – were ranked among conurbations of more than 100,000 people. Seaside resorts were, in effect, major English towns – and yet they were quite unlike any other towns of comparable size.

No amount of census detail could hope to convey the essence of a day or a week at the seaside. For the armies of English people who flocked to the coast throughout the 1930s, the seaside resorts continued to provide the unique pleasure and variety which their parents had found before 1914. The lure of the sea and the beach remained much as before, but the *style* had undoubtedly shifted – a shift registered in photographs and in those unique barometers of seaside tastes and fashions, the comic postcard. The harsher, less sympathetic view of working people, so common in the pioneer cards before 1914, gave way to a more benign view. The postcards showed cheekiness, rudeness, sexual innuendo – and undoubted class overtones. But the postcards of the inter-war years reflect a more relaxed holidaying public which, during a brief respite by the sea, felt themselves to be the equal of their social superiors, untrammelled by the restraints of work or industry. There is, however, strong evidence that the cards appealed to people whose lives were dominated not by the sun, but by the grimmer realities of urban and industrial life:

Enjoy yourself lass! You'll have to do as the buzzer says next week.

I hear you're swanking about but don't forget you've to come back to earth.

'Coming back to earth'; 'the call of the buzzer', these were warnings of a harsher, more important life waiting miles away from the coast. But, despite the recurring reminders of the working world, the comic postcards of the period exude enjoyment, good health and, to a degree, permissiveness. Vulgarity had, of course, long been a prominent element in postcards – in common with other forms of graphic commentary on seaside life. As early as 1913 *The Times* reported: 'Attempts to check that trade in vulgar and semi-indecent postcards by police action had already been made at Manchester, Hastings and some of the manufacturing districts of Lancashire and Yorkshire.' Postcards, like stage shows and the new films, were to continue to provide watch-committees with something to froth about for years to come. An earthy vulgarity – best represented by the work of Donald McGill – continued to run as a theme through seaside postcards, and it stands as a visual reminder of this important element in popular culture (which can be equally captured in music-hall songs, jokes and oral culture). But the cards were often an insight into an outsider's view of working-class life, both at the seaside and at work, for it is clear that, although the postcards sold in their millions, they were not products of working-class life.

With a few miserable exceptions – the hen-pecked skinny husband, the fat, funereal, dominating wife, the bawling children ('He's got lungs of leather and bawls like a bull') – postcard people enjoy themselves. We can hardly expect the seaside industries – of which the cards were a part – to convey a miserable impression of the resorts, but the overwhelming image of life at the resorts is that there was fun for all. And the fun available had markedly changed since Edwardian England. There appears to be more fun on the beach itself. The ranks of over-dressed Edwardians hiding from the sun give way, by the late 1920s, to more unrestrained groups of pleasure-seekers, sprawling on the sands and in their deck-chairs, generally exposing themselves to the sun. Indeed, one recurring image of the postcards from the inter-war years is the large round lady, dressed, if that is the word, in a swimming-costume which reveals her ample proportions; the rear views of large ladies and the skeletal remains of their husbands stand revealed, in the new-style bathing-costumes.

At this level, the postcards merely confirm what we know from photographs and the history of fashion – that styles of beach- and swimming-wear changed, largely as a result of the major changes in social attitudes. Edwardian women hid beneath their clothes; after the war their clothes revealed their figures. The briefer, more manageable swimming-costumes (for men and women) were relatively cheap, and could be donned on the beach, behind a towel, or worn underneath the clothes. Swimmers could henceforth change on the beach without the burden (and expense) of bathing and changing machines and booths. Dressing and undressing in public came to be accepted as a ritual of seaside life.

The new briefer costumes were ideal for sunbathing, and the cult of sun worship, noticeably absent in pre-war days, became a dominant feature of seaside life. Indeed, so important did sunbathing become, that local authorities began to publicize their town's sunshine statistics. Climate thus came to be a key-factor in enhancing a resort's appeal but, for the great majority of holiday-makers it was to be many years before they could choose to follow the sun, since they were tied by time and finance to the more familiar resorts, close to home. It was of little use to Lancastrian textile workers to know that Bourne-mouth had more hours of sunshine than Blackpool, for they were in no position to do anything about it. And, in any event, the power of social traditions drew them to the Lancashire coast. For those with the time and money, however, sunshine statistics undoubtedly came to exert great sway – drawing them ever further, south and west, across the Channel and to the Mediter-ranean. The flight to the sun had begun.

Much of the inspiration for sun worship had come from France and, gradually, the sun-tan became the most desirable of summer complexions. Whereas Edwardians had prided themselves on pale rosy complexions, by the late 1920s a tan was much more socially acceptable, and the creams to prevent the sun from harming the skin were superseded by sun-tan lotions. Swimming also became more fashionable, and, to make it more comfortable, resorts invested heavily – yet again – in new pools (often open-air). There was a nationwide vogue for modern swimming-pools – the Lido in London's Serpentine being perhaps the best remembered – and thousands flocked to them whenever the summer sun broke through. For increasing numbers of people, holidays were now planned with the aim of following the sun – and getting a tan. Even those who continued to visit their favourite resorts, stripped off and exposed themselves to the sun, a fact regularly noted in comic postcards. Ironically, this cult of the open air (like camping) was given an added boost by the German 'Strength through Joy' movement.

* * *

Between the wars there was, as before, an amazing variety of entertainments available at the seaside. But their style was modernized in the 1920s, rapidly losing its Edwardian flavour, and quickly absorbing the fads and fancies of a new generation. Ever more troupes, 'concert-parties' and artistes came under the management of theatrical agencies (who provided them with work in other parts of the country when the summer season ended). Among holiday-makers it was perhaps the seaside concerts which made the greatest impression – largely because they were family affairs. Children did not, of course, visit the music-halls, and, in general, only went to the theatre for the pantomime. But the seaside shows provided genuine family entertainment – and hence they remained a fond memory of a seaside visit from one year to another. Moreover, in terms of the survival of live, national entertainment, the seaside theatres and shows became all the more important in the inter-war years because of the collapse of the music-hall – a collapse which was under way before 1914 but effectively completed between the wars.

The most significant cause of the decline of the music-hall was the impact of the cinema and the wireless. Seaside towns, like towns everywhere – were soon provided with those red-brick monuments of inter-war film-going, and in many towns the standard design of the Odeon cinema became a characteristic feature of English architecture in the 1930s. Often the new cinemas were merely adaptations of older theatres and music-halls and, both for this, and for that other new vogue of the inter-war years, ballroom-dancing, the resorts were ideally suited. But, in addition to the converted buildings, large chains of companies built new dance-halls in the resorts and in all the major English cities. In a sense, seaside life, with its general lack of conventional, workaday modesty and restraint, was ideally suited to the rather frenetic dancing of the 1920s. People on holiday relaxed and, away from the constraints of the home environment, they enthusiastically joined in the dances which called for a vigorous lack of bashfulness. Young people might perhaps have been prepared to do the Charleston at the local Palais in, say, the East End or Oldham, but at the seaside even the older visitors could join in without fear of appearing ridiculous or being frowned upon by friends and neighbours.

Dancing was yet another new feature of the process of mass, commercial leisure which cut across class lines and which developed rapidly after the First World War. One historian of dancing has noted: 'The process of "democratisation", or provision of inexpensive facilities for dancing, went on apace throughout the twenties . . . gradually all the urban centres and holiday towns came to have excellent facilities for social dancing.'

Dancing was soon a prominent feature of working-class life, in the industrial cities and in the seaside resorts. Dancing among the upper classes (though they were often the first to adapt the more 'daring' North American dances which were denounced by surgeons and bishops in *The Times*) generally took place in the small private ballrooms of hotels, restaurants and clubs, while working-class dancing evolved in the large modern dance-halls. The result was that 'ballroom dancing came to be in inverse proportion to social status'. Dancing, which lasted throughout the evening and into the night, soon became a feature of trips to the seaside, and in the summer months the resorts were able to attract the best-known bands (whose fame was further increased in the late 1920s by the new B.B.C.). So popular was ballroom-dancing that many people, particularly those who were now made more mobile by the new fad of motor bikes, travelled to the coastal resorts simply for an evening's dancing.

The coming of the B.B.C., wielding, from the first, a formative influence on cultural trends, helped to promote the resorts even further, for the B.B.C. frequently broadcasted concerts and light music from the still-flourishing resort pavilions. For a century, music had characterized the seaside summer, and between the wars this feature remained as strong as ever. The B.B.C. helped to extend, and in some cases create, new vogues and tastes in popular music. Resorts could of course afford to pay the ever-rising fees of top bands, orchestras and conductors, simply because they had a guaranteed market among their millions of visitors. Nor was the music simply lightweight and 'popular'. In 1926 the Llandudno Pier Company appointed the young Malcolm Sargent to take over their orchestra – which he did to stunning effect. The more 'residential' the resort, the more 'serious' the music of local orchestras; the latest tunes from Harlem were unlikely to appeal to the retired folks of Eastbourne or Bournemouth. But the more popular resorts attracted the orchestras which formed the backbone of B.B.C. light musical entertainment. And it could be argued that by broadcasting music from the resorts and bringing familiar tunes into the home, the B.B.C. helped to increase the seaside's attractions. It is revealing, for instance, that Reginald Dixon's organ music became a major feature of B.B.C. radio for many years. Clearly, there was nothing specifically seaside-like about orchestral music played in the 1930s, much of which could be heard in any city in the land, but the fact that it came from the seaside was sufficient to enhance its appeal. The organ of the Blackpool Tower sounded very much like any other organ, but to the audience grouped around their new wireless sets, it evoked memories of visits to the sea.

Resorts were ideal locations for other new fads of the inter-war years, particularly car-rallies and air-shows. For the new cars – in a society in which commercial pressure cultivated a commitment to speed – the promenades made ideal display and racing surfaces. Understandably, local authorities were keen to attract such events. But these rallies and races, and the illumi-nations which seaside towns introduced in order to extend their limited season, often placed extra financial burdens on the thousands of local residents, who received little in return for their troubles. The resorts were commercially minded towns where municipal authorities spent millions of pounds of rate-payers' money to enhance their commercial appeal. But the beneficiaries of these investments were often not the residents, but those commercial groups with powerful influence in the towns. Spending £3–£4 million each year, seaside authorities were even more promiscuous than most authorities in spending other people's money.

By the mid 1930s the summer movement of people to the coast had reached epic proportions. Blackpool attracted 7 million between June and September; Rhyl $2\frac{1}{2}$ million; Redcar 2 million and even the 'quieter' resorts of Morecambe and East-bourne attracted 1 million visitors. A town-planner of the period labelled the process: 'that democratisation of the coast which set in with the coming of the railway'. In the process, however, as more people travelled, with more money to spend, and as communications enabled people to travel farther and farther afield, there was a drift of the better-off to the south and west – and of course to Europe. It is significant that the most intensive seaside development of the 1930s took place in Devon – at Plymouth and Torquay – primarily for those in search of quieter spots well away from existing resorts, which were increasingly under siege from tourists and trippers. Few resorts were, like Scarborough, able to accommodate different social classes in an almost compartmentalized fashion. On the whole, the resorts reflected the basic class divisions of society at large, and when a resort became too 'plebeian' in tone, its more genteel visitors moved elsewhere, a tendency which had been pronounced since the early days of the railways. Town-planners of the 1930s, moreover, *assumed* that resorts should be zoned on fundamentally class lines; presuming that the social and re-creational needs of the different classes were both different and conflicting. One noted: 'Scarborough has natural barriers which separate her classes of visitors, and although such differences as exist today are fast disappearing they are still very strongly marked. Those responsible for the development of Scarborough should keep these distinctions in mind.' It seems ironic that a process which, time and again, was described as 'democrat-ization' and which involved the extension of holidays to more and more ordinary working people, resulted in a confirmation of traditional holiday patterns. It is a very revealing insight into English society on the eve of the Second World War that contemporaries assumed that holidays were as segregated as English life in general. Moreover, there was a widespread assumption that this situation was correct; was as it ought to be. Holidays, like sports, housing, work and, to a degree, even religion, were mirrors which offered an image, sometimes dis-torted, of a society fundamentally divided by class. The war of 1939, however, demanded a national effort. It was, as Angus Calder has written, a people's war; a conflict which required a united effort of all groups. The old social divides were no longer adequate for the task ahead.

7 $\infty\infty\infty$ *From Austerity to Prosperity*

$\infty\infty\infty$ The Second World War was a conflict not merely between the armed forces but also between the civilian populations of the belligerent powers. While the military losses were not to be as devastating as in the conflict twenty years before, war was soon to launch destruction, as never before, on civilian populations. The aeroplane had come of age and it was immediately realized that most parts of Britain were exposed to the terrors of aerial attack. War had been expected for some time before the outbreak of hostilities and it was, from the first, appreciated that this time there would be no artificial divide between armed forces and civilians. Two areas of the country were particularly vulnerable: the cities and industrial areas were exposed to air attack, while large stretches of the south and east coasts seemed provocatively exposed to the threat of invasion.

Long before hostilities began in earnest, $1\frac{1}{2}$ million women and children had been moved from the dangers of the cities to the relative safety – but unwelcoming rigours – of an evacuee's life in the country or on the west coast. For many evacuated children, the unpleasantness of their adopted homes remained among the most formative of their wartime memories. In the first three days of war, Blackpool took in 37,500 evacuees from nearby industrial cities – an achievement described by a local newspaperman in a vein of proud, civic romanticism. The evacuees 'accepted war without a murmur, saw the sea – some of them for the first time – rode down the Promenade to their billets, and, after the narrow cobbled streets of their own towns and the smoking factory chimneys, came into Blackpool as if into a new Eden.' Small Jewish boys from Manchester re-

membered, however, not the 'Blackpool rock' thrust into their
hands at the Central Station, but the pork sausages thrust down
their throats by insensitive foster-mothers.

Seaside resorts which had in peacetime attracted the holiday
visitor took on a new, wartime appearance. Some, like Blackpool, found their population swelled by evacuees. Others on the
Essex, Kent and Sussex coasts were equally swiftly denuded of
their populations and fortified against a threatened invasion.
Piers were blown up, beaches barricaded and draped in barbed
wire, bays were mined and headlands turned into observation
posts and gun emplacements. The gaudy, painted face of seaside
England soon peeled and weathered – or was reduced to the
greys, greens and browns of a nation at war. But some of the
relatively safe resorts were ideally equipped for absorbing
waves of urban immigrants, and no sooner had the first waves
of evacuees settled down than the civil servants began to arrive.
With dozens of hotels and boarding-houses, and their thousands
of spare beds, the resorts were well suited for the relocation of
government ministries moved out of the threatened capital.
Hotels became government offices and landladies found themselves catering for civil servants, who, like the evacuees, often
found their enforced accommodation unsatisfactory. Boarding-
house shortcomings, tolerable when shared by one's family in
summer, proved intolerable in the lonely freezing winter of
1940.

Plentiful accommodation at the resorts also attracted the
armed forces, now compelled to push through a crash programme of expansion. Blackpool soon housed 45,000 R.A.F.
personnel, scattered among 5000 houses, and while it is true
that tens of thousands of men were billeted in towns throughout
the country, resorts were best suited for such rapid influxes.
Indeed, after the Dunkirk evacuation, Blackpool's military
population shot up from 45,000 to 70,000. Blackpool had more
to offer the military than beds, however, for the promenade was
a ready-made drill and parade ground. It has been calculated
that more than $\frac{3}{4}$ million R.A.F. recruits received their basic
training in wartime Blackpool.

Seaside towns had been built to provide for the pleasure of
transient holiday-makers. Ironically, many of the town's basic
attractions were easily converted to the task of running a

military machine. Blackpool became a virtual military camp. Troops trained on the beach and prom, and took over the Winter Gardens, the Olympia, the Opera House and the Empress Ballroom. Ballrooms became gymnasiums and assembly halls, and where dancers had once shown their paces, thousands of men now displayed their kits. The uniforms on display were not only British; with the presence of *émigré* European forces and, later, the massive build-up of American and Commonwealth troops, Blackpool became cosmopolitan. Some of the town's entertainments continued in the evening (even when a hall had been used by the military during the day). Boredom, that occupational disease of armed forces, even in war, could be contained by female company and the military in Blackpool were lucky in having on hand the female workers employed in the nearby aircraft factories. Unhappily for the British troops, it was often felt that the local girls found the American troops' extra cash more attractive. Understandably, perhaps, it was claimed by more penurious troops that contemporary female utility knickers were generally too loose: 'One Yank and they're off'.

Blackpool seems to have retained its vitality throughout the war, partly due to the happy accident of geography, but other resorts fared badly. Margate, which seemed to blink across at Nazi Europe, became very run-down. In August 1943, at what should have been the peak of the summer season, a mere two hotels and four boarding-houses were open, though this was scarcely surprising considering the enemy's hit-and-run tactics and the town's exposed position. Some people were able to visit certain resorts but, on the whole, holidays by the sea remained remote dreams for most working people. Long working hours, punitive taxation, strict rationing of food and petrol, rigid control of public transport, cumulatively made holidays on the pre-war scale a practical impossibility. Moreover, large areas of the coastline were out-of-bounds to the civilian population. The Isle of Man, once a playground for the north and Scotland, was turned into a large-scale prison-camp for suspects whose only crime was to have been born abroad.

The war years saw, inevitably, little effort to stop the material decay of the resorts, and yet it was clear to many people that, although holiday resorts might appear low on the list of post-war priorities, the physical and spiritual well-being of a people sorely tried by six years of war would require swift and urgent attention. And, as if to give warning of the nation's intentions, when an austere peace returned in 1945 there was a massive upsurge in pre-war leisures – most noticeably with football and visits to the seaside towns. Victory in 1945 saw new attitudes manifesting themselves among the British people, exemplified in the political lurch towards a Labour Party with an ambitious programme of post-war reconstruction. Socially, too, demobilized troops (and civilians slowly released from directed labour) wanted both a change from the inter-war years, and an extension of the emergent leisure which many of them had just begun to experience before the war. Significantly, Labour's Election Manifesto of 1945 included plans for holidays. Despite the slightly battered face of the post-war resorts, the summer season of 1945, beginning only a few weeks after the German surrender, saw record crowds pouring to the coast. On that first July Wakes holiday in 1945, the trains carried 102,889 people to Blackpool on one day alone – an all-time record. Happily, the British did not have to fight on their beaches but they celebrated their victory by flopping on them.

People had not forgotten pre-war attractions and pleasures and, although scarcity and rationing continued to characterize the British way of life into the 1950s, seaside resorts could at least offer that range of cheap attractions and pleasures which first attracted urban people in the previous century. Despite the austerity, it was ironic that many of the thousands flocking to the coast had more money to spend than ever, and this was particularly noticeable among demobilized troops anxious to make up for lost time. Lots of people had money to spend, but there was often little to spend it on; at least at the resorts they could find guaranteed enjoyment – and the seaside towns continued to live up to their fame for relieving people of their money.

The most important post-war social change in holiday-making was the dramatic upsurge in holidays with pay. The legislation of 1938 had only begun to make an impression at the outbreak of war, but by 1945 some 80 per cent of the work-force were paid to take their holidays. But the central problem – discussed at length by social investigators in the last years of the war – remained the familiar one of how best to bring holidays within the reach of poorer groups. Suggestions ranged from direct government subsidies through to nationalization of seaside and rural properties to provide for the poor. Such ambitions were, inevitably, to remain unfulfilled, though the slow diffusion of better material prosperity in the 1950s enabled more and more people to take holidays. The difficulty of the problems is well-illustrated by the fact that even today the poor tend not to take holidays, and it seems that no amount of theorizing will alter the situation. Little, short of unpredictable massive social and economic change in British society, seems likely to change it.

Soon after the war, it was pointed out that holiday resorts presented unique social and economic problems for any government, though their needs were overshadowed by the more obvious demands of war-worn industries and cities. They suffered heavy winter unemployment, particularly among women, they were important to society as a whole, and yet were in desperate need of post-war capital investment. The resorts formed, quite simply, a distinct, and not easily appreciated, light industrial area, which like other areas of industry were of legitimate concern to a government anxious to get the country back on an economically sound, and socially healthy, footing. But who could expect a beleaguered Labour government to consider the special economic plight of towns whose rationale seemed to be the pursuit of pleasure, at a time when the nation was faced with the stark prospects of post-war survival? The truth of the matter was that the seaside towns had been too effective in their own propaganda, for, having convinced the nation (often through their municipal publicity departments) that the resorts were the embodiment of pleasure, it was difficult, in the late 1940s, to argue that they were, equally, important areas of economic activity deserving of government help and consideration. When, in the early 1950s, the resorts were able to shake off their severe post-war gloom and to take on the trappings of material prosperity, they were to do so not through government assistance, but through the well-tried seaside combination of interested capital and municipal encouragement. Once again the financiers and entrepreneurs moved in – as they had whenever the resorts offered scope for commercial investment – to enhance the towns' appeal. Municipal help often took the form of councils dominated by men with local trading and commercial interests, who were anxious to further their own town's attractions through municipal investments of ratepayers' money. The fact remains that the revival of the seaside towns was made possible, not, as commentators had hoped in the mid 1940s, as part of a government-sponsored industrial revival which would also bring social equality, but by the self-interested efforts of capitalist investors. In the 1950s, as in the 1880s, the seaside towns offer a case study of the consequences of English entrepreneurial capital at work. But, in the late 1940s, until the nation could emerge from its more serious economic dislocations, there was little chance of a major change in seaside fortunes and the history of the resorts tended to be a continuation, in an exaggerated form, of life in the 1930s.

Resorts experienced boom conditions in the late 1940s and there is a beguiling similarity between the peak years of travel to the resorts and attendances at football matches – both activities reaching a peak in 1948–9. In 1949, for example, Scarborough had its record number of visitors arriving by coach – in excess of ½ million; the year before, an unsurpassed 625,000 travelled to the Isle of Man (the numbers declining steadily thereafter). But the *patterns* of holiday-making remained remarkably durable. People tended to follow the routes established in pre-war days, although the geographic spread of holidays was increasingly noticeable as transport – and finance – opened up areas of the country previously monopolized by wealthier visitors. By the summer of 1949 it was calculated that some 30 million people were seeking holiday accommodation on the coast (though as many as 15 million people were still obliged to stay at home during their holidays), but often in more and more secluded places. In 1949 *The Times* noted: 'Working class families – having largely driven the middle classes out of popular large resorts, and having pursued them into smaller, more select seaside towns – are beginning to join in the general search for small, quiet "unspoiled" holiday centres, both on the coast and inland.'

The debate about holidays in 1937–8 had often focused on the serious problems caused by congestion in the narrow period given over to the summer holidays. Ten years later the problem had become even more acute; 'the need for spreading holidays ever more evenly over the summer months, and even by shifting the bank holidays, has become acute only during the past decade.' Whereas *The Times* noted that one half of families on holiday would, ideally, have liked self-catering accommodation on the coast – presumably for financial reasons – other evidence paints quite a different picture. A survey in May 1949 for *News Review* showed that married women were keener than other groups on traditional seaside holidays. 'Oh! how I would love the rest!' sighed one housewife. While husbands doubtless appreciated the savings of a self-catering holiday, wives clearly found the 'inclusive' holiday, where the landlady did the hard work, the most attractive of all. It was significant, for instance, that the survey found 'loafing' on holiday more common among the old, and women. Men were finding themselves ever more liberated from their jobs – or rather, they were given more free time and spare cash – but their wives remained tied to the onerous tasks of household and family life and, not surprisingly, working-class housewives regarded inclusive holidays by the sea as *the* great break from domestic routines, which changed only when children left home.

Aspirations and plans for annual holidays – about where to go, what to do, how to save, what to wear, how to travel and dozens of other details – often occupied people's thoughts and actions in the long periods between the summer holidays, though, for the fortunate few (13 per cent in 1948), two holidays were becoming common. Memories of an earlier holiday – captured by holiday snapshots – and plans for the coming summer meant that the holidays occupied more than a mere week or two in people's annual routines. Just as the ghosts of Christmas past and future ensure that Christmas lasts longer than a few days, so too did the *idea* of the annual holiday become a common preoccupation, a process encouraged by the advertisements of commercial organizations, travel companies and the resorts themselves. Clearly, this had been true throughout the history of seaside holidays, but the quantum leap in holiday taking and the rise in national expectations, further enhanced the national commitment to the annual holiday. The growing assumption that a holiday was a part of the year's cycle must have made the inability to afford such a holiday all the more intolerable. Furthermore, seaside holidays were ideally suited to children (the timing of the holiday season remained inflexibly linked to the rigidity of the school system). And yet three quarters of those families with more than three children were, as late as 1949, forced to stay at home during their holidays. And it was significant that very few people interviewed for a survey, in that same year, wanted to take their holidays without their children. Then, as now, and in the 1880s, the most important determining factors governing the popular holiday, were the economic facts of life among working people.

Even poverty (and its frequent bedfellow, large numbers of children) could not prevent people from daydreaming about holidays. Of those interviewed by Mass Observation in 1949, three quarters expressed a desire to go abroad. Of these, 39 per cent wanted to go to Europe, 11 per cent to the U.S.A. and 23 per cent to the Far East or around the world. This was of course long before the travel-industry and the airlines had begun to convince the public that the world is indeed their oyster, and it suggests either a degree of dissatisfaction with existing holidays, or an innate desire to see the world (a desire more than satisfied for thousands of men between 1939 and 1945). Whatever the cause, people's holiday aspirations far outstripped their economic potential. Only a very small percentage who had taken seaside holidays in 1948, and planned to do so again in 1949, would have repeated the holiday if they had an alternative. That they, nonetheless, returned, time and again, to the seaside resorts gives some indication of the powerful fusion of traditional cultural patterns and economic constraints.

The post-war years witnessed a revival of the holiday camps, which had established themselves in the 1930s. Despite the proliferation of camping organizations, Billy Butlin, by virtue of his remarkable flair for publicity, was able to capture the public imagination to the extent that his name became synonymous with holiday camping. The virtue of his camps was the never-ending whirl of activity and events, designed to occupy visitors of all ages throughout their waking hours; there was always something to do from early morning to late at night. For those who could tolerate the congested blur of noisy communal life, the main objection was cost. At £1 per day, in 1947, the camps attracted mainly middle-class visitors; it was calculated that a mere 5 per cent of the visitors were working class in that year, and the dominance of middle-class holiday-makers can be gauged by the presence of 500 cars in Butlin's Pwllheli car park – an early date for widespread car-ownership.

In the late 1940s, outside opinion was concerned about the possible fall from moral grace at the holiday camps, and whereas it is true that the holiday resorts had, since the late nineteenth century, been the objects of hostile moral and ecclesiastical concern, the camps presented an even sharper image of easy-living. One social investigator, spurred by the self-confessed ambition of discovering whether the camps were good for the social and moral life of the nation, discovered that standards of sexual morality were high (except among the staff), a fact which he attributed to the dominance of middle-class holiday-makers. Fornication was presumably kept within marital bounds. Less pleasing, however, was the amount of beer-drinking at the camps; a Methodist minister to one camp in 1947, was appalled to meet a man wearing a badge proclaiming himself to be the 'Champion Beer Drinker'. As private establishments, the camps avoided the constraints of English licensing laws, and the apparent ever-open bars impressed on hostile observers the image that the campers floated through their holidays on a soothing tide of beer. It is true that holiday camps depended on the proceeds from the bars (and snack bars) to raise their narrow profit margins (thus making camping-holidays even more expensive), but there is little evidence to suggest that drinking was a 'problem' in any other way than the traditional offence it caused to prickly Nonconformist consciences. As if to confirm the prejudices of the theologically inclined, a survey suggested that 67 per cent of holiday campers were not regular church-goers, though at one camp, a chapel was built for the faithful, on a convenient site, sandwiched between the beer store and the cycle shed – a symbolic representation of the age-old struggle by salvation against damnation and recreation.

Billy Butlin was an undoubtedly brilliant pioneering publicist and, whatever outsiders felt about his camps' shortcomings, he built up a widespread and committed clientele who regularly returned to his camps. In the 1940s and 1950s, visitors to the camps seem to have repeated the patterns of visitors to the resorts; once a holiday spot had been tried and enjoyed, it became part of a regular routine. It seems ironic that holidays which were a break from the sameness of everyday life, them-selves became part of a wider annual routine. Not until the privately owned car became a feature of English society did these traditional migratory patterns of the English people begin to change – and then only slightly.

Butlin hit upon the clever idea of nurturing holiday memories by regular reunions during the winter months. Throughout the late 1940s and early 1950s his organization provided large-scale reunions in the major cities so that holiday friendships and acquaintances could be renewed, and plans laid for future visits. There was even a Butlin's campers' service in St Paul's Cathedral, though it is not immediately clear why the Anglican authorities should have lent themselves to so blatant a piece of commercial-ism. In the face of such aggressive commercial ventures – at a time when drabness and austerity were national hallmarks – it is scarcely surprising that Butlin's, and holiday camps in general, produced a furore in newspapers and journals among people whose views of holidays were quite different from the com-mercial world of the camps. For those leisured critics whose holidays generally consisted of self-organized, self-improving visits to European cities, or invigorating walks over hills and mountains, the cacophony of commercial noise and music – smacking as it did of the 'B.B.C. Light Programme and Ameri-can Cinema' – was anathema. They did not understand, or approve of, holidays in the mass – and the holiday camps presented a concentrated form of mass holiday which, it was claimed, exploited 'the indolence of people who want a holiday but are too lazy to organize it for themselves'. Whenever the English people have found ways of enjoying themselves in the mass – even though encouraged to do so by powerful commercial interests – their social superiors have found ample reasons to criticize their behaviour. At play, as at work, the English have traditionally gazed at each other in bemusement across the cordon sanitaire of English class-lines.

One index of changing social patterns among English holiday-makers was the slow emergence of car ownership. In the 1930s the number of private cars on the roads had doubled from 1 to 2 million, but in the years immediately after the war the private car remained a luxury (their scarcity reflected in their relatively high second-hand value), and trains continued to take the very great majority of trippers to the coast. Slowly, however, the statistics changed, as road transport began to make massive inroads into the railway's dominance. In 1947, for example, the percentage of holiday-makers going to Skegness by various routes was as follows: by car 17 per cent, by bus or coach 16 per cent, and by train 67 per cent. Four years later the number going by train had fallen to 47 per cent, the rest was evenly divided between cars and coaches; but by 1955 the three forms of transport were almost evenly divided. At the same time as the resorts began to suffer the serious problems of traffic congestion, many of their connecting railway lines, once their umbilical cord to the supplies of visitors, began to decline and wither. But the summer flow of road transport to the resorts brought those towns, once again, to the attention of the town-planners.

The post-war boom in seaside holidays was largely made possible by the extension of holidays with pay. Whereas in 1951, 61 per cent of manual labourers were entitled to two weeks' holiday with pay, by 1955 this had increased to 96 per cent; twenty years later the movement was towards three and four weeks' holiday with pay. But, by the mid 1950s, the overall holiday statistics hid distinct holiday patterns. Often the statistics merely confirm what common sense suggests: for instance, that holiday-makers were more common among those aged between sixteen and twenty-four, between the ages of twenty-five and thirty-nine holiday-making was less common, but it revived again among those over forty. Clearly, the commitments of family life took their toll of potential holiday-makers. Among the retired, however, only one in three went for a holiday. The patterns of the mid 1950s seem little different in rough outline from the pioneering days of popular holidays in the previous century. Although London attracted the largest single group of holiday-makers, the resorts were still able, in the mid 1950s, to lure 65 per cent of all holiday-makers. The sheer numbers involved were enormous. Blackpool attracted 7 million people in the season and could accommodate ½ million overnight at any one time; Brighton could put up 200,000. Such figures give an immediate sense of the enormity of the popular movements to the coast. But such numbers placed enormous strains on the social and urban facilities of seaside resorts. Transport was only the most obvious problem facing the resorts, and the authorities had to put a great deal of planning, and even more money, into the provision of water, sewage and cleaning, while other amenities – gas and electricity, for instance – had also to be provided for the towns' large transient populations. But to provide such costly amenities for a mere three months in the year involved heavy expense, again of the ratepayers' money, which in no way benefited the resident population during the other nine months. Once again, residents of seaside towns found themselves subsidizing – to a fairly massive extent – the short-term pleasures of holiday-makers. Entrepreneurial guile and know-how were more than adequate for satisfying the recreational demands of holiday-makers, but that could take place only within the wider framework of municipally organized and financed urban development.

Not all resorts faced large-scale invasions of tourists. Indeed, the popular idea of a resort – of Blackpool, Southend or Brighton – distorts the overall, seaside picture, for of the seventy-plus resorts, very few were large-scale towns able to double their populations overnight. Compared to Blackpool's 7 million visitors, the 50,000 to Aberystwyth or 40,000 to Bognor Regis seem inconsequential. But each resort had (and has) its own peculiar charm and its own, often regional, committed visitors. Indeed, so varied is the face of seaside England, that it often seems that the only common denominator shared by all the resorts is their closeness to the sea. Despite their great differences, commentators continued, throughout the early 1950s, to group them together as Dr Granville had done more than a century before. Some still regarded seaside towns as 'health resorts', comparing them to the older inland spas. Even the modernization of English society which became noticeable in the early 1950s, failed to alter some of the old, ingrained attitudes towards the seaside towns, and some people persisted in viewing the resorts in the vein of Edwardian England. A publication of 1952, celebrating its fortieth birthday, talked of the holiday towns as if no new strides in medical science or social custom had taken place since the magazine's first publication. Aberystwyth was thought good for 'nerve exhaustion' (though colleagues who once taught at the local university would disagree), while Anglesey was claimed to be good for 'the prolongation of weakened lives'. To the south, Barry, it was alleged, was of no help to those with catarrh, rheumatism or asthma. That Blackpool was described as 'the chief watering place of Lancashire' would have made little sense to the millions who trekked westwards from the textile towns in search of something quite different. In many respects, the 'popular resorts' were vastly different from those seaside towns thought to be 'health resorts', not simply because of geographical location, but primarily because they appealed to distinct and different social classes.

In so far as the resorts provided visitors with an invigorating change of scene and air, they could all claim to be health resorts. Bournemouth was, however, more specifically and more obviously a health resort than, say, Blackpool. Towns like Bournemouth were – in conception and development – health resorts, and had heavy concentrations of old people and private nursing-homes, with the attendant strain on local social services. But even these resorts became highly popular resorts in the summer season. For many English people, seaside life meant the quiet restfulness of Bournemouth, or Hove, or increasingly, Torquay – and not the gaudier face of the popular resorts.

If we concentrate on the seaside towns in the first decade after the Second World War, it seems difficult to believe that the country was in the grip of serious economic troubles. Record crowds, the volume of money flowing into the resorts, growing competition between road and rail and the rapid re-vival of seaside entertainments – all suggest a prospering economy. The real picture was of course quite different, and it seems that, as in the case of cinema and football, the resorts thrived in inverse proportion to national prosperity. The harsher the times, the more intent people seemed to have been on enjoyment, and the more determined to spend their spare money on having a good time. Seaside towns in the late 1940s had the added attraction of a thriving black market, which provided visitors with a number of luxury and essential goods without the necessary ration coupons.

The economic forces which had helped to shape the popular holiday in late Victorian England – the embryonic consumer power of working people – were functions of better times.

When, after 1945, people flocked to the coast as never before, the economic climate hardly seemed suitable for a spending-spree. But the fact that one took place suggests the national determination to be rid of the restraints and frustrations of wartime. It seemed pointless to make huge sacrifices to win a war if the years of peace were to bring nothing more than a repetition of wartime conditions. Moreover, it appears that the Labour government's constant exhortations to continuing sacrifice became counter-productive. In the upper reaches of the government and civil service there was a powerful puritanical streak which regarded the nation's leisure as unimportant; a marginal issue to the central drive for economic recovery. But, in almost every area of leisure, the people asserted their own contrary views by enjoying themselves whenever the opportunity arose. The determination to watch football, visit the seaside, go to the cinema – or whatever – in the post-war years was itself an indication of the enhanced status of leisure. People were obviously no longer satisfied merely to have regular work and a decent wage; they also wanted more, paid leisure time and, as the nation moved into a new economic phase where fuller employment and rising living standards were to become the norm, the emphasis upon leisure time and holiday entitlement became an important negotiating point between management and labour.

Seaside resorts were boom areas while other sectors of the economy faltered. Those resorts with large entertainment industries profited by the national spending-spree. In 1948, for example, the Blackpool Tower Company was able to pay a dividend of 35 per cent, and the town's fifteen cinemas and fourteen live theatres were similarly booming. Stars who made their names on the halls, or more recently on radio, found, by the sea, a ready summer market for their talents. Once again, as before 1914, the popular resorts provided that unique variety of entertainments so sought by holiday-makers. But all this was to change when, from the mid 1950s, a new wave of unprecedented consumer power led to the emergence of new entertainments, which eliminated much of the seaside variety. London-based organizations and conglomerates swept away many of the theatres and cinemas, replacing them with newer, more lucrative entertainment centres.

In retrospect the years immediately after the war present an unusual picture: a hang-over from pre-war Britain which was, in leisure terms, overthrown by the rise of what contemporaries called prosperity. Many of the forms of leisure – of which seaside holidays were the most extreme – were, by now, traditional pastimes. Cinema, radio stars, ballroom-dancing, evenings of organ music, live theatre – all had been equally prominent in seaside life before 1939, and it was natural that, as soon as possible, those aspects of seaside life should be revived to cater for the massive numbers of visitors. Indeed, the very rush to the sea after the war was an affirmation of the old traditions of enjoying oneself on the coast. And people did so in unparalleled numbers – almost because of the hard times.

It is impossible to pinpoint exactly when post-war austerity gave way to rising material prosperity. Some people made fortunes in the years of post-war hardship, and millions more remained poor while society was becoming more prosperous. Prosperity was not an immediate, all-embracing movement; it was like the slow thawing and break-up of an ice floe. There are a number of indices to material prosperity: T.V.- and car-ownership, real earnings, the rapid further expansion of holidays with pay, consumer durables and cultural fads. But, through it all, the seaside holiday remained secure – though not unchanging. While other mass cultural forms changed dramatically – football, cinema and the church, particularly, under the pressure of economic decay – the seaside towns seemed best able to adapt to the new economic forces. Seaside resorts had, throughout their history, proved remarkably durable and adaptable, in a strange transmutation from pre-industrial watering places to the playgrounds of millions of urban people. That adaptability was to stand the resorts in good stead in the next twenty years, as society around them began to undergo revolutionary social changes.

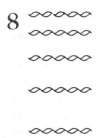

8 More Prosperous Times

The increased consumption of material goods and the rise in real wages, which are generally taken to represent widening prosperity, had begun to transform the face of English society by the mid 1950s. Prosperity became a fact of English life, and the national commitment to it was largely responsible for the Conservative election victory of 1959. It may have been a political gimmick to tell the British people: 'You've never had it so good', but it was accepted as a truism by the electorate. Bland assertions that Britain had become an affluent society on the American model, inevitably ignored those residual layers of poverty which seemed all the more offensive in lying unflinchingly in the midst of rising general well-being. There was nothing new about this of course for, as we have seen, the slow and sometimes faltering rise of popular consumer power over the past century had been similarly pockmarked by periodic, regional or cyclical poverty. In 1959, no less than in 1879, it offered no comfort to the poor to be told that many of their contemporaries were becoming more prosperous.

As the fifties gave way to the sixties there were, nonetheless, signs of rising general affluence; an affluence reflected in the most startling fashion by the dramatic rise in car-ownership, the possession of a T.V. – and the explosion of foreign holidays. Each of these features of modern English society entailed a number of changes in life-styles and attitudes; T.V., for instance, helped to kill off thousands of cinemas, while the car made most parts of the country accessible to the public. Equally, however, each innovation was itself made possible by a complexity of changes, with firm historical roots. The boom in foreign travel was made a possibility – in a technical sense – by the arrival of mass air travel, by the consequent lowering of air costs (arrested by the oil crisis of 1973) and the proliferation of companies providing cheap inclusive 'package' tours to a number of European resorts. But, it is very striking that the development of the new pleasure grounds of Europe, in general, took place by the sea. It was as if the 1960s saw a repetition of the nineteenth-century pattern: whereas the railways opened up the English coast for urban people, the airlines forged similar links to the warmer waters of the Mediterranean.

A foreign holiday was a remarkable new venture for many millions of English people, though the English had long been a familiar and distinctive sight in Europe, particularly at the Edwardian spas and the south of France. The 'Grand Tour' of the eighteenth century had polished the education of the sons of the aristocracy, but it was, again, the railways which opened up large regions of Europe to the curious gaze of the newly enriched English middle class in the following century. In search of new excitements, anxious to escape from the increasingly popular resorts at home, or, in many cases, desperate to lengthen their enfeebled lives in the mountains or on the coasts of Europe, the English middle and upper classes, Baedeker in hand, headed across the Channel in growing numbers. The boom years were 1870–1914 – coincidental with (and to a degree, repelled by) the flood of English visitors to the English coasts. Between 1890 and 1900, for example, the number of passengers sailing to Europe grew from 418,000 to 669,290; by 1914 it exceeded a million. In these years the British left their permanent mark, especially in France. To this day, the names of the hotels in the south of France and the northern ports: l'Angleterre, Britannique, Londres, Windsor, Prince de Galles, stand as monuments to a bygone age of English social dominance. By the time of the First World War, tourism from Britain to Europe – like holidays in Britain itself – had become a major industry, which throughout Europe was, according to an economist, 'the fruit of a liberal expansionist economy based on technical and industrial progress'.

Expensive European holidays were generally the preserve of the better-off, both before and after the First World War. In the condescending words of an earlier commentator: 'As for the manual workers – they were still marooned on their island. It would be many years before they left it – and then they'd be wearing khaki.' Oddly enough, it was the surviving sights of the Great War which began to draw English tourists across the Channel after 1918 – despite the newly introduced passport. New travel firms – led by George Lunn – heavy advertising and the touring potential of the motor coach, led to a post-war boom in European travel, often to places which had until recently been inaccessible. Motor transport opened up Switzerland, for example; and, following the departure of the occupation forces in 1925, there was a similar travel boom to Germany. By 1930, the numbers travelling to Europe had almost reached the one-million mark, but the economic crash led to a collapse in holiday-making in Europe in the early 1930s, and the English middle classes turned once again to local resorts for their holidays. Bizarre as it seems, in retrospect, from the mid 1930s there was a revived interest in Nazi Germany, due in part to the advertisements which declared Germany to be 'The Land of Dreams Come True'. Not for the last time, the publicists and apologists were successful in nurturing tourism in a country built upon bestialities.

The curiosity to see the ruins of war was not repeated after 1945, and, in any case, the country was too poor to allow its citizens to export local currency. Henceforth, the Treasury had a major say in the evolution of foreign travel, an important indicator of the size and the economic importance of overseas travel. Often absurd, and more often counter-productive, financial limitations on foreign travel have punctuated the history of British travel over the past three decades. But the massive growth in foreign holidays since the late 1950s, has been seriously hindered only by the economic recession of the 1970s. For those able to afford it, the flight to the sun, or the gruelling car-ride south, have become as indispensable as their father's and grandfather's early trips to the English seaside.

It was no accident that the new resorts which began to seduce millions of English holiday-makers, especially in Spain, were seaside towns. The Mediterranean countries could, of course, offer more or less guaranteed sunshine, but it was as sunny inland as on the coast. The truth, however, was that, for the English and for many other Europeans, a summer holiday was synonymous with a trek to the water's edge, be it sea, lake or river. Holidays were characterized by the sea and, for those pioneers keen to lure northern Europeans south in the summer, it was essential to create holiday facilities on the coast. Nowhere were the consequences of these summer migrations more staggering than in Spain where, in a decade, a string of major cities sprang up along the Mediterranean shoreline. In the early 1930s a mere ¼ million visitors had travelled to Spain each year. When, twenty years later, Spain began to recover from the devastation of the Civil War, some 2 million tourists holidayed in her cheap sunshine; by the early 1960s, however, this had grown to 12 million, four fifths of whom settled on the beaches of the Costa Brava. The number of Britons travelling to Spain grew enormously. In 1964 the figure stood at 709,000; nine years later it had risen to 2,775,000 – 1 million more than the numbers travelling to Spain's nearest rival, France. The days had clearly gone when an English monarch could reject the idea of a foreign visit with the terse line: 'Abroad's beastly.'

Sunshine became a powerful factor of holiday-making in England between the wars; in the 1960s and 1970s it has become the most important attraction of most European resorts. Nor was the lure of the sun unique to the British, for the diffusion of prosperity throughout western Europe since the late 1950s has led to the emergence of tourism as a major European industry, to the extent that there are an estimated 400 European resorts with a total resident population of 12 million – which doubles in the holiday season. By 1958, in Britain alone, it was calculated that the tourist trade employed 5 per cent of the working population. Holiday-making – in all its forms – is clearly a major industry, so much so that foreign visitors to Britain have become a vital part of the nation's drive for foreign currency.

The English holiday by the sea, along with many other forms of mass leisure, underwent considerable changes in the 1960s and 1970s. Almost three quarters of the 30 million holiday-makers who stay in Britain, continue to head for the sea. The actual numbers taking annual holidays have not changed substantially since the early 1950s (five in ten in 1951; six in ten in 1970), but it is very noticeable that a growing number of people (4½ million in 1962) enjoy two holidays each year.

Moreover, many more people have chosen to live by the sea; today, the coastal dwellers constitute some 5 per cent of the country's population and, although a considerable number are elderly and retired, substantial numbers are there to cater for the millions of visitors.

Many holiday-makers continue to travel to the coast by train, except of course in those areas where the swingeing axe of Dr Beeching lopped off whole lines, in the 1960s. But it is motor transport which has, more than anything else since the coming of the railways, reshaped the direction and pattern of the English holiday. It is often claimed that the car offers its owners an extension of their homes, by providing an extra room with a changing view, and this comment seems amply justified by the degree to which people use their cars simply to see the coast or country, without stepping outside to sample the fresh air. For the planners, municipal authorities and police, the movement of millions of people by car has presented problems on an unprecedented scale. Of course, the impact of the private car has had major repercussions on urban society throughout the world, but the British resorts, and other leisure attractions, have had to face a distinctive and seasonal traffic-problem, though the flow of summer traffic to the coasts has also created major problems for those towns and areas *en route*, between the major cities and the resorts, which now find themselves engulfed at summer and Bank-Holiday weekends. Ring-roads and by-passes, motorways and diversions, all have become part of the scenery on the way to the sea – often as far back as fifty miles from the coast itself. Tadcaster and York have traditionally stood as obstacles to the traffic between the Yorkshire industrial towns and the favourite seaside resorts on the Yorkshire coast. Preston has similarly defended Blackpool against the traffic from other Lancashire towns.

Nowhere, however, has the flow of holiday traffic created more serious problems than in the West Country where a growing number of vehicles finds itself squeezed into inadequate roads, strung between congested towns. The only solution has seemed to be the construction, at enormous expense, of new roads and motorways, roads which devour the very attractions many of the visitors want to see. Despite common protestation to the contrary, the private motorist eats up millions of pounds of national resources (many times more than the nationalized railways), without adding very much to the general social good. The private motor car has come to dominate not simply roads and cities but also an undue share of the nation's finances. Whereas it is clear, for example, that trade and business will benefit by the new motorway links to Blackpool, or the new motorway slowly nosing its way through the West Country, it is, nonetheless, true that their rationale and justification is the need to cope with a seasonal flow of traffic which is acute only for a very brief part of the year. Holidays by the sea now pose serious problems, which the resorts themselves are unable to solve, though, in a muted form, this has perhaps always been true. The stampede to the railways on the first Bank Holidays in the 1870s bears all the hallmarks of the modern rush to the sea in cars. Though separated by a century, both represent a society capable of releasing its members *en masse* for the pursuit of leisure.

One by-product of the advance of the private car was the rash of caravan parks which erupted around the coast, creating still further difficulties for those concerned about the slow erosion of the shoreline by urban development. For the holiday-maker, however, the caravan has undoubtedly created new holiday dimensions. Caravans have substantially increased the volume of holiday accommodation, much of it away from the traditional resort-centres. Near Scarborough, caravan-sites have created an extra 5000 beds, all of which are primarily self-catering, with consequent repercussions on the older patterns of inclusive accommodation.

One of the most notable changes in the resorts has been the relative decline of traditional board-and-lodging holidays. Fewer people go to boarding-houses – large numbers of which have been converted into self-catering flats. But it is the caravan, both in fixed sites and towed by owners, which has made the major inroads into the old patterns of accommodation. In 1955, 2 million took their holidays in caravans; by the late 1960s this had risen to $4\frac{1}{2}$ million. In 1955, caravan holidays accounted for only 8 per cent of the national total, but by 1970 they had reached 18 per cent. But the most far-reaching result of the caravan has been, not the changes in accommodation, but the further erosion of open space by the proliferation of caravan-sites. In addition, the congestion and driving-difficulties produced by touring caravans are obvious on any summer road.

Self-catering and caravan holidays have made possible the growth of holidays in particular regions, particularly the south-west – where the increase in holidays has been greater than the national average. But it is to Wales that we must turn for the full impact of caravaning, for there, at Abergele and Porthcawl, for instance, we find a concentration of caravans which produces a truly urban density of population. In Wales, some 34 per cent of all holiday accommodation is provided by caravans, and the explanation is relatively straightforward, taking us back, once again, to the wider problem of communications. Many of the Welsh areas opened up to the holiday-maker by car and caravan were undeveloped by the railways, or, where railway connections existed, their links to the major conurbations were too tortuous and time-consuming for effective holiday travel. The pioneering treks to the coast were made by day-trippers, and as long as such trips to the Welsh coast were either impossible or difficult, the tradition of holiday-making was difficult to establish. But the coach and later the car overcame these difficulties and brought parts of north and mid Wales within relatively easy access of the towns and cities in the English Midlands. One result has been the establishment of parts of the Welsh coast as the 'natural' resorts for the Black Country. The variety of Midland accents is as familiar and commonplace on the mid Wales coast in August as the accents of Lancashire at Blackpool, or of York-shire at Scarborough.

Self-catering holidays have experienced a boom in the past decade – to a degree encouraged by the independence bestowed by the car, and, at first sight, these holidays seem to have ful-filled the expectations expressed in the 1930s and 1940s. Then, however, the main purpose of the self-catering holiday was seen to be the creation of holidays for the low-income groups, but, today, many of the self-catering holidays are enjoyed by those with cars, caravans, or complex and expensive camping-equipment. A number of seaside city-centre flats clearly cater for low-income groups, but the self-catering holidays on camp- and caravan-sites at the edge of the resorts, or even in new, isolated, self-contained locations, are a symptom both of rising material prosperity and of greater mobility among large groups of English people. While it is no longer true that car ownership is a sign of personal prosperity (except in the sense that the very poor are, in general, denied the material benefits which others take for granted), it is now the most important index to holiday-making. Something like three fifths of all English holiday-makers take their holidays by car. Car ownership itself is another indicator of a mature industrial society, in which the luxuries of yesterday have become today's essentials. Equally dramatic has been the expansion of holidays with pay. On the eve of the Second World War, a mere forty years ago, the state made its first major concession (apart from Bank Holidays) to the idea that paid holidays were the right of all working people, and yet by August 1974 the paid-holiday entitlement of working men had increased three- or four-fold; 37 per cent enjoyed three weeks, 54 per cent between three and four – and the drift is towards even longer paid holidays.

Despite the diffusion of holidays – of changing, newer, and more expensive holidays – throughout the English population, there still remain major exceptions. This is, after all, characteristic of the history of holidays over the past century, and, in a crude way, it simply reflects the differences between the poor and the better-off. A sociologist has explained that in 1970, 20 per cent of the highest socio-economic group (AB) failed to take a holiday whereas among the lowest (DE) almost 50 per cent had no holiday. Similarly, of those who enjoyed more than one holiday, 56 per cent belonged to group AB (which itself comprises only 14 per cent of the population). But the claim that, 'the propensity to take holidays varies directly with social class', is merely an unnecessarily complex way of saying that the poor have fewer holidays than the better-off – hardly a surprising discovery.

It is, however, worth examining the related sociological observation that working-class holidays are often characterized 'by a high degree of organisation, collective orientation and passivity'. Although it is not clear what 'passivity' means in this context, it is certainly true that 'organisation' and 'collective orientation' are historical features of working-class holidays. Holidays were locally or communally defined and enjoyed, but this pattern has been severely fissured by the impact of car ownership. Another important solvent of the traditional working-class community-holiday has been the rapid decline of some of the major industries which spawned the great holiday breaks of the late nineteenth century. King Cotton, for instance, has lost his crown, and the traditional Wakes weeks of many cotton towns are now pale reflections of their former selves.

We ought not to be suprised that the new holiday patterns among working people – the package tour, caravan-site or camp-site – seem to be following in the wake of the more prosperous middle class; this, after all, has been the traditional development of the English holiday. But this is not to claim that the modern working-class holiday is simply a pale reflection, or even a deliberate imitation, of the cultural patterns established by other social groups, for the popularizing of holiday-making is just one aspect of a wider cultural diffusion which, by virtue of changing economic fortunes, has enabled more and more working people to enjoy facilities and customs previously beyond their economic reach. But, in seizing the leisure opportunities which came their way – for the first time in the years 1870–1914 – working people imposed their own social style upon the seaside holiday, as they did upon association football (which was transformed from a public-school game into the national game of working men). By the turn of the century, English working people had come to colonize and, in some cases, monopolize certain seaside resorts. Though it may be true that many working people today enjoy holidays, which in their parents' and grandparents' generation had been the preserve of the better-off, there can be no mistaking the differences in social tone which continue to differentiate the leisure pursuits of different social groups.

The luxury of being able to pick and choose between different resorts depends largely upon a visitor's finances, and, until recently, such a range of choice was beyond the resources of most working-class visitors; this factor above all others propelled people towards resorts in their own region. But the widening of choice among working people – itself a function of growing consumer power – and the impact of the car, have brought many more resorts within the reach of working people. Nonetheless, it is noticeable that the resorts have succeeded in maintaining their appeal to visitors from their traditional catchment-areas. It may well be that people's attitudes towards the seaside have become so solidly ingrained as to render them impervious to attractions elsewhere.

Sunbathing, swimming, and lounging on a beach are now essential attributes of a seaside holiday, but the statistics on climate do not seem to have undermined the attraction of the colder northern resorts. Weather statistics prove conclusively that the south coast enjoys more sunshine than other coastal areas. Brighton, for example, has 256 hours more sunshine each year than Blackpool. But, whereas Brighton attracts 4–5 million visitors, Blackpool continues to boast of 7 million. Moreover, the English continue to flock to the coast in their greatest numbers in August, although that is not the best English summer-month for low rainfall and plenty of sunshine. In deciding when, and where, to go on holiday, the English have had their choice fixed by a complex historical process, which to this day remains remarkably powerful. It is true, of course, that for many people, particularly those with a car, the weather is now an important factor. If the day's weather forecast predicts gloom along the coast, it is scarcely worth setting out for a day's trip. On the other hand, even the brightest of weather forecasts will scarcely persuade people to drive 300 miles from Yorkshire to the south coast rather than, say, to Scarborough. People tend to plan their holidays well in advance, knowing that in their limited free time there will be severe competition from tens of thousands of people for space and accommodation. When arranging an English holiday months ahead, there is no guarantee that the weather will be fine – even in resorts thought to be 'sunnier' than others. Even those who decide to use their homes as a base for a series of day-trips often make that decision well in advance, though for them, it seems that the daily weather forecasts are important. Overall, however, it is not clear how climatic considerations determine the English holiday, except of course in extreme cases – in an exceptionally wet summer, fewer people will visit the resorts. Conversely, we know that many people resolve their doubts about the English summer by flying to the Mediterranean.

English seaside resorts have, since the inter-war years, spent large amounts of money in promoting their sunny image but it is unclear how such publicity has altered the contours of English holiday-making. Although it is true that many more people have turned to Spain and other European resorts, the statistics of visitors to the English coastal towns scarcely suggest a collapse in their popularity. (Furthermore, the idea of holidays at 'home' has been revived in the 1970s by force of economic hardship.) The figures for visitors to the resorts in the mid 1960s remain impressive: Blackpool 7 million, Brighton and Hove 4–5 million, Hastings 3 million, Bournemouth and Southport 2 million, Scarborough 1 million, Eastbourne 1 million.

English resorts differ greatly from one another, but the nature of social life at the more popular resorts has remained remarkably steady, despite the impact of prosperity. The 1960s and 1970s have seen a continuation of the process, first discernible a century before, of commercial changes slowly reshaping the physical face of the resorts, in order to provide visitors with what they wanted and were familiar with. Certain features remain apparently unalterable. The English seaside is unthinkable without donkeys, buckets and spades, ice-cream and sea-food stalls. But the commercial face of the popular resorts has experienced major changes and, in the 1960s and 1970s just as at earlier periods, seaside commercial entertainment has been a barometer of cultural change. T.V. has transformed seaside entertainment – as it has revolutionized so many areas of modern culture; and it is worth noting that the T.V. companies present a number of shows and 'spectaculars' direct from the seaside.

The impact of T.V. on seaside entertainment is similar to that made, in the previous century, by the music-hall. Before the First World War, the major resorts were able to attract highly paid music-hall stars; today, the new stars of T.V. also find themselves drawn to the resorts in the summer. It is an important guide to the power of T.V. as the pace-maker of popular entertainment, that the entire casts of T.V. series are nowadays transferred to the seaside theatres in the summer. The seaside visitors want – yet again – not the new and unfamiliar, but the known and proven; and the resorts give them what they want. Yet for many people in the theatre the summer season is vital, for, in an age where live theatre has declined substantially and where T.V. – and the clubs – offer the only alternative business, the shows at the seaside towns remain among the last strongholds of live, light entertainment.

Today, outside agencies tend to control the full range of

seaside entertainments. The agents, companies, theatres and piers, often belong to, or are controlled by, major theatrical or property companies based in London. Seaside entertainment is an aspect of metropolitan-controlled show business which cares little for a particular resort – save its ability to yield the requisite profits. There has often been an element of outside business-interest in the resorts, but in the first wave of seaside popularity before 1914 much of the initiative in local entertainment came from local men. One result of outside financial control has been the ravaging of seaside architecture (though in this the resorts share the fate of all English Victorian cities). Many of the piers, which continue to function as leisure centres, have lost their original faces beneath plastic reconstructions. At the same time, property companies have also stimulated the national craving for gambling (a change made possible by the relaxation of national gambling-laws). All English cities now have the apparently ever-open arcades where a range of machines and gadgets wait open-mouthed for the visitors' spare cash. Inevitably, gambling-arcades find abundant custom in the resorts, where they have established themselves as features of sea-front architecture. So, too, have the bingo halls which, though commonplace throughout the land, find in the resorts some of their prime positions and an even more guaranteed prosperity.

There has been an amazing development of entertainment gadgetry at the seaside. New materials and cheap forms of manufacture have enabled the leisure industries to 'develop' whole sites at the resorts into new fun-palaces, which house a range of technical innovations. Just as the heavy, ornate, filigree iron- and wood-work of Victorian and Edwardian architecture gave way, between the wars, to a plywood veneer, so, in the past fifteen years, much has been levelled in order that new structures of foam, plastic and polythene can take their place. Moreover, the pace of urban reconstruction is accelerating – under the constant pressure to modernize and create new attractions. The end result is the regular and thorough redevelopment of seaside towns. Visitors, returning after an absence of twenty years, are greeted by virtually different towns, although urban renewal is no worse at the resorts than in other English towns and cities. The resorts, however, represented, in many cases, classic examples of Victorian and Edwardian architecture and style (particularly in their theatres, piers and hotels), and it is consequently all the more important to preserve them.

One of the most important social changes in English cultural patterns since the early 1960s has been the proliferation of restaurants and eating-places – frequently pioneered by the Chinese. The resulting expansion of eating-houses and the national chains of restaurants, have found a suitable market in the resorts. But this is not a complete innovation, for cooked food had long been available at the seaside. Before 1914, working-class visitors were faced with a greater variety of cheap, cooked food than they could ever have found in their home towns. In the same way as gambling and entertainment, however, catering has now entered the world of big business and, in conjunction with the national desire to drink, has led to the establishment of large numbers of seaside restaurants. These, like cars, costly shows, expensive drinking habits and gambling saloons, are signs and symptoms of a society with a large amount of surplus cash readily available for the pursuit of leisure. Resorts are, of course, in essence, urban monuments to the pursuit of mass leisure; more recently, however, that leisure has become more varied, spectacular and colourfully seductive.

While historians have, in general, been slow in responding to the interesting story of the seaside holiday, there has been a great deal of curiosity shown by social geographers, sociologists and economists, largely because their disciplines have been affected directly by the consequences of holiday-making and tourism. In 1975, visitors to Britain spent more than £1000 million and, by any standards, it is clear that the holiday business has become a major British industry. In the process, however, the consequent overcrowding of tourist attractions has led to demands for restrictions on tourism, despite the great profits for the country. Even the untrained eye can detect the consequences of holiday-making, which threaten to destroy the very amenities which lure tourists in the first instance; and the 1970s have seen a repetition of those alarmed cries from conservationists, which first became noticeable among town-planners in the 1930s. Countryside, coastline and water are threatened by the sheer weight of numbers disgorged in the summer, by the explosion in building and by the ubiquitous motor car. Although these problems exist throughout the country, it is still the case that the greatest weight of holiday-making continues to fall upon the seaside and the roads to the coasts, for 75 per cent of all English holidays are still taken by the sea. And whereas it is true that the south, from Kent to Cornwall, has increased its relative share of visitors, it is the apparently unchanging nature of the English migrations to the seaside which are striking. Professor Patmore, the most prominent contemporary scholar to study the social geography of holidays, has noted 'the obvious tendency for an area to be most attractive to those who live nearest to it.' And this pattern was no less obvious a century ago.

There can be no doubt, however, that the modern holiday has created new problems over the past twenty years – and has accentuated older difficulties. One result has been the introduction of legislation to curb the worst ravages of holiday development (controls first demanded by the town-planners of the 1930s). Yet the holidaying instinct of the English people now threatens to engulf far more than the coast in the summer season; with the greater flexibility of the car and coach, millions of tourists are deposited in the nation's rural beauty-spots. Most of the National Parks, like the coast, are within easy reach of the major towns, and the tides of people which sweep through the parks in the summer indicate the growing complexity of modern holidays (and the rural challenge to the seaside towns). But in this overcrowded land, where, since the coming of the railways, the cities have been easily linked to both country and coast, this variety of out-of-town travel has always been available to the city-dweller. The great change of the present day is that many more people are able to afford such visits and holidays. With the diffusion of consumer power and the improvement in road transport (offset by the contraction and expense of the railways), English holiday-makers now pose serious challenges for both planners and conservationists. Certain areas of English holiday-making seem to have become self-consuming, and one does not need to be a prophet of impending ecological doom to appreciate the threat posed by the holiday-makers to both the English coastline and the countryside. Nor is this threat merely a pro-

duct of population-growth, for it is primarily a result of prosperity – of the liberation of the majority of an advanced in-
dustrialized population for the pursuit of leisure. The pattern is
much the same throughout the western world, but it is one of
the great peculiarities of the English that, despite the changes,
they continue to enjoy the seaside pleasures which first attracted
their forbears a century before.

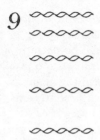

To claim that the English seaside holiday was created by changes in English social and economic life does not tell us a great deal about the resorts themselves, or about the vast differences between them. On the surface, their history appears to be beguilingly similar, but it takes only a few cursory visits to the coast to appreciate that the differences are more striking than the similarities. Why, for example, is Bognor so much less plebeian than Southend? Why have Scarborough and Brighton been able to maintain their appeal to visitors from various social classes? One thing seems clear, however; whenever we can detect such differences between resorts, it is certain that we can trace them to basic historical forces.

Seaside resorts are united by their common historical reliance on communications with the major cities. Indeed, their history can often be written in terms of the changing methods of transportation. Margate, Gravesend and Southend emerged as early seaside watering places because they were easily reached by boat down the Thames. In other cases social pressure led to the creation of good overland routes. Once Brighton had established its claims as a resort of royal, aristocratic and fashionable pretensions, its coach routes to London improved markedly. In 1835, 117,000 people travelled to Brighton by coach, but fifteen years later the railways whisked 73,000 visitors to the coast in a single week. In 1862, 132,000 travelled to Brighton by train on Easter Monday alone. The railways, of course, revolutionized most areas of English society, but their full impact was particularly obvious in the post-railway development of seaside towns. New railway links between the inland towns and the coast, transformed sleepy fishing villages (Blackpool); planted cities where nothing existed before (Bourne-mouth) or boosted flagging seaside towns (Brighton). Thriving seaside towns, realizing the even greater economic potential of a railway link, fought to bring the railway – and the crowds – to their doorstep. In Scarborough, the railway lobby overcame the opposing isolationist lobby. Within a week of the opening of the railway, excursionists began to descend on the Yorkshire coast; 1000 from Wakefield, a week later, a contingent from Newcastle: 'the pale, emaciated inhabitants of murky and densely populated cities seeking to restore their sickly frames to health and vigour by frequent immersions in the sea.' Further north, the shipbuilding- and fishing-port of Whitby resisted the seductions of the railway, but the town's slow economic decline finally forced its authorities to compete with their Yorkshire coastal neighbours for the train-borne tourist trade.

A number of today's resorts scarcely existed before the coming of the railways – often at quite a late date. In such cases, the example of resorts which had already boomed on the crest of railway development, proved important in persuading local pressure-groups to seek both a railway link and the consequent encouragement of seaside visitors. The east-coast towns of Skegness and Mablethorpe – insignificant villages until the 1870s – were brought within the national railway-network between 1873 and 1875 by the determined cooperation of the railway companies and Skegness landowners. There immediately followed an urban revolution – and waves of summer visitors from the nearest conurbations in the east Midlands. By 1913, only forty years after the first railway links, ¾ million visitors sampled the Skegness air, an upsurge which paralleled the development of Bournemouth.

In the century between the 1840s and the 1940s, the history of the resorts was first shaped, and then dominated, by the rail-ways, which formed the vital life-line to the cities. Whenever a resort needed an added economic boost – in the form of extra visitors – they had to petition the railway companies. In 1891 Blackpool tradesmen petitioned the local railway companies, 'with the object of giving facilities to tradesmen and others in inland towns to visit Blackpool in the middle of the week'. Earlier, in 1882, when Skegness took the decision to advertise its charms in the towns of the Midlands, it did so in the local stations and railway hotels.

Where railway lines did not exist, resorts were keen to get them built. Why was it, for example, that Blackpool – almost as close to many of the Yorkshire towns as the more popular Scarborough – failed to attract a large number of Yorkshire holiday-makers? After all, Blackpool is seventy-nine miles from Leeds – seven miles nearer than Scarborough. But, in fact, the railway connections were much more complicated and time-consuming, and by the late 1930s plans were discussed, 'to improve the road connection between Leeds and the Fylde coast as to place its holiday resorts and their surroundings on equal terms with their competitors on the opposite side of England.'

The railway companies did more than ferry millions of people to the coast, for they frequently invested heavily in the resorts' urban development. The railway stations, and near-by railway hotels, became centres of seaside life, and the social and re-creational facilities catering for the trippers tended to develop close to the station, and between the station and the beach. But the railway companies were beset by the same difficulties which troubled local municipal authorities; namely, how best to provide for the enormous demand in a narrow summer season – and on Bank Holidays – when the 'normal' traffic was infinitely lighter. Not only did this involve careful planning and marshalling of rolling-stock and staff in August, but it required the provision of large numbers of platforms at the seaside stations – and even special stations – most of which could be used only in the summer. To this day, Scarborough has nine platforms to cope with the summer traffic – but most stand silent in the winter.

The railways' most vital cargo to the coast was the people – the visitors for whom the resorts were developed and whose spare cash was so important. For a century the railways monopolized this traffic, and not until the 1950s did they find their passengers seduced away to cheaper, more flexible road transport. Throughout that century of rail dominance, the railways found themselves carrying ever more people to the resorts; quite simply, because the population was growing, at a time when a growing proportion of that population found itself keen and able to visit the coast.

Among the most durable features of the English rush to the sea has been its timing – and that timing is, to a large extent, a historical accident. The very great majority of English people have taken their holidays in July and August, not necessarily because those are the best weeks for holidays but because the holiday-making traditions developed around those weeks. In industries – like the textile-trade – with traditional annual holidays, the tendency towards 'bunching' the holidays in July and August was exacerbated by the development of holidays with pay, and compulsory schooling. It was logistically easier for some firms – and in some cases, whole towns – to close down operations for one or two weeks, thus creating congestion on the local railways and local resorts. And, by the late 1930s, this congestion was taxing the railway companies and the resorts to the limit. On the eve of the Second World War some form of staggered holidays – with all the attendant complications – seemed essential. But when peacetime holiday-making resumed, the patterns remained much as before, and the amount of post-war 'staggering' was only marginal. Whereas in 1951, 64 per cent of the British took their holidays in July and August, it had only fallen to 61 per cent by 1960; by 1973 it stood at 62 per cent.

Geography and distance have been consistently important in shaping the contours of English holiday-making. Working people first visited the coast on day-trips, which, having established a tradition for visiting a particular resort, later expanded into longer visits. To put it simply, visitors came from those towns and cities which were close and which were suitably placed for a day-trip. Again, it is remarkable that the connection between visitors and the resorts has remained durable to the present day – even when visitors travel to the coast for longer stays. For more than a century, the evidence has remained consistent; the largest single proportion of visitors to most English resorts come from a specific catchment-area. Blackpool was the seaside Mecca for the textile towns of Lancashire, and a regional-planning report, as late as 1937, took it as axiomatic that it was from 'the Lancashire cotton operatives' that 'the visitors to the Fylde Coast are so largely drawn'. From one resort to another, this pattern has remained similar. Scarborough's first excursionists in the 1840s came from Yorkshire and the north-east – and that connection has endured into the twentieth century. Excursionists, by train or car, must clearly come from within a reasonable 'commuting' distance, but what is unusual is the degree to which long-stay holiday-makers come from the same region. Long after coach and car transport had begun to make inroads into the railway monopoly to the Lincolnshire coast, the largest proportion of visitors continued to come from the Midlands. The cumulative effect is that holiday-making has tended to be a highly regional affair (though this syndrome has begun to show fissures in the recent past, especially with the development of the West Country holiday resorts). But one half of the visitors to Scarborough and Whitby still come from the north; and, in 1962, one half of the visitors to Wales came from the north-west and Midlands.

One useful rule of thumb is to see the country as divided into a number of regional holiday-catchment-areas, which feed primarily into local resorts. These regions correspond, roughly, to more substantial contours of industrial and urban life. Moving from north to south, the first most obvious subdivision is the north-west region which has traditionally turned to the west-coast resorts, from Morecambe down to New Brighton and into North Wales. Yorkshire and the north-east have their own line of coastal towns which stretch south to the Lincolnshire border. Those living in the north Midlands – from the Potteries south – tend to look to North Wales and both the Lancashire and Yorkshire coasts for holidays, and, although, since the 1870s, the east Midlands have turned to the Lincolnshire coast, the Midlands proper have traditionally regarded Wales and the West Country as their particular holiday area. London and the south have found their holiday resorts along the coasts of Essex, Kent and Sussex. More recently, however, there has been the development of the south-west region as a distinct holiday area, attracting visitors from all parts of the country. With the exception of this last – and latest – holiday area, English holiday statistics have consistently shown that the resorts' largest single group of visitors have come from within their 'home' region. There are, inevitably, exceptions, which have grown in number and size with the diffusion of prosperity. But there have, perhaps, always been trippers and holiday-makers anxious to head *away* from their workmates and neighbours.

To talk of holidaying-regions is, in many respects, a bland, unsatisfying way of analysing holidays, for it tells us nothing about particulars and peculiarities. Once we probe below the surface of these regional patterns, it becomes much more difficult to explain why certain resorts came to exert enormous sway over particular towns – and over particular social classes within those towns. Morecambe was never able to challenge the dominance of Blackpool, and Whitby failed to erode Scarborough's pull, because their railways came too late. Timing was clearly essential in the establishment of a resort, and often a new challenger found that by the time it had developed its urban and recreational facilities, an older regional rival had begun to exert an almost orbital pull over the industrial hinterland. Once people had sampled a particular resort, their visits rapidly became part of a tradition; elements in an annual culture which were not to be easily dislodged by similar, though unproven, attractions near-by. Resorts which did develop at a late date, and which flourished, were generally able to do so because they had no obvious or similar rival. Such was the case with Bournemouth, Skegness and Mablethorpe.

There are, however, certain anomalies which defy simple explanation. Why did Blackpool become plebeian, but Southport more respectable and middle class? Blackpool's Town Clerk complained in 1939: 'I am afraid that in the past, Blackpool specialised principally on the provision of facilities for working class visitors staying a week; the lower class weekenders and day trippers.' The reasons behind this problem are complex, though, as Professor Perkin has shown, land-holding was clearly very important. Southport was designed on a grander scale with larger land-holdings, intended to prevent that rash of cheap speculative building which, in its turn, attracted the entrepreneurial interests and the working-class visitors to the resorts. On the other hand, Skegness was also planned and laid out on a grand scale and with an overall design in mind, and yet Skegness was to attract quite different visitors. From every viewpoint, Southport – larger and older than Blackpool – seemed ideally placed to attract the Lancastrian working-class holidaymakers. And yet it did not do so in significant numbers.

Similar examples exist throughout the holiday regions, yet it is very difficult to pinpoint their exact genesis and progress.

What are needed are comparative studies which trace the dynamics of seaside development. But one feature seems to stand out, above all others, namely, the weight of cultural tradition. Visits to a resort became part of people's lives. Released from work together, working people travelled to the coast as groups and even as whole communities. Personal recommendations and experience swiftly established the appeal – or unattractiveness – of a resort, encouraging friends, relatives, neighbours and workmates to sample it. It was also important that working people travelled to the seaside in a collective manner because, in the company of their peers, they were able to enjoy a strange environment. Plans for visits were laid and discussed well in advance and money was saved through a variety of community schemes. Travelling itself was important; the journey to the coast was part of the holiday – the first taste of a more carefree existence, away from industrial routines – and from the first descriptions of railway excursions in the 1840s through to the 'chara' trips of the 1930s, the image is remarkably similar: of people who work with, or live close to, each other, having a good time *en route* to the seaside.

The day – or the week – at the coast was also punctuated by contact with neighbours and friends, inevitably, as long as holidays remained unstaggered. Favourite boarding-houses, pubs, spots on the beach, and shows, were shared, not simply with the family but also with other people from the home town. It is noticeable, for instance, that many of the favourite comedians, who starred year after year at the resorts, appealed directly to the home-town peculiarities of the audience; the banter, jokes and anecdotes flung at the audience frequently involved a particular town – though the comedian would change the town as the audience changed. On the whole, however, these regional comedians died under the glare of national T.V. coverage; residents of Tunbridge Wells do not, in general, understand jokes about Blackburn. It was simple of course for a north-country comedian to know, for example, during Blackburn Wakes week, that jokes about that town – often delivered with minute social and geographic detail – would go down well with his audience. Thus, seaside entertainments often reinforced the audience's sense of 'being at home'.

This sense of ease – of familiarity, even when far from home –

was an important ingredient in establishing a resort's customary appeal among working people. For people whose lives were dominated by a harsh industrial and work discipline – and all within a narrow geographic focus – it was important that new pleasures should not be totally strange, unexpected or unfamiliar. Visiting the seaside, like other aspects of English working-class social life (such as football, the church, music and the variations of street life), evolved not as an individual but as a collective experience. The seaside trip became part of working-class rituals – an experience to which people aspired, even when they could never hope to afford it. Though the seaside trips differed from town to town, the overall pattern was very similar, and by the 1890s had become a prominent feature of working-class social life – and was to remain so until the present day.

Visitors returned time and again, and the regular migratory patterns were a distinctive aspect of English holiday-making. Before 1914 the tripper paid annual pilgrimages to the same spot. Between the wars, good landladies could be guaranteed the same 'crowd' year after year – hence the importance of booking well in advance, often at the time of leaving one year, to return the next. When holiday camps made inroads into the holiday market after the Second World War, the sequence of events was the familiar one (encouraged by the management), of visitors returning year after year. Whether the holiday-makers' insistence on returning to the same place has any general significance (a need, perhaps, to stick to the familiar, on the part of people whose lives were organized down to the last detail), it is difficult to judge. But it is clear that these routines cut across class lines. Working-class holiday-makers insisted on the same well-tried landlady; middle-class visitors paid return trips to their favourite camps.

There was, of course, yet another distinct pattern, and that was the flight of others *away* from the mainstream of holiday-makers. Pushed out of the old watering places by the middle and then – worst of all – the working class, the upper classes drifted first to the inaccessible parts of Britain, particularly to the south-west; later to Europe, notably to the south of France; and, later still, to the most distant and inaccessible points on the networks of British Airways. With the coming of the car and cheap jet-travel, the wealthy have virtually abandoned whole areas of Britain to the intrusion of the popular visitor, contenting themselves with rural retreats and far-flung excursions.

It seems, then, that one factor which helped to establish the dominance of one resort rather than another, among working-class visitors was the town's suitability for day-trippers. Before 1914 the great majority of working-class visitors to the coast went for the day, and for them the availability of cheap accommodation was not really important. What mattered (much more than land easily converted into cheap accommodation) was the presence of hawkers and entertainers. Clearly, cheap land was an attraction to those wanting to erect stalls and booths to cater for the trippers, but the encouragement given to such catering by municipal authorities (and the police) was equally important. Yet many of those catering for the visitors did so illegally, without licence or approval. Again, it reminds us that the problem is circular; what economic circumstances made it apparent that such commercial activity was worthwhile? Did the entertainers and hawkers attract the visitors – or did they flock to the coast knowing that the trippers could provide them with a livelihood?

The outcome is clear. By the 1890s the individual character of the resorts had been established, to remain in a similar mould for years to come. Blackpool was plebeian – and its tradesmen saw its future inextricably bound up with the fortunes of the working-class visitors. Margate, once 'respectable', had become plebeian. Brighton – always fashionable – was 'common' only in bursts. Southport – with its air of residential gentility – still made provision for working-class visitors, which enabled the two societies to coexist, at a distance from each other. Each resort was distinct and unique.

Although certain resorts were dominated by visitors of one social class, some seaside towns continued to appeal to all. Scarborough and Brighton, in particular, were able to have the best of both worlds, possessing a resident population which was distinctly upper class and yet attracting the annual droves of more plebeian visitors. Scarborough seemed ideally placed, for it could cater for different social classes in distinct geographical areas – a fact much praised by its town-planners of the 1930s: 'Of Scarborough it may be said that, owing to its natural divisions, it is better able to entertain all classes than any other seaside resort in England.' Even at the height of the season it was possible to escape from the bustle and throng of the main beach by moving to the south shore and esplanade – the focal-point during the town's more respectable past. It is a very different story on the opposite coast at Blackpool where, in season, it is possible to escape from the noisy crowds only by travelling some miles south to the more peaceful – more middle-class – residential resort of Lytham.

But at Blackpool, Scarborough or Brighton, the weight of historical continuity is much more striking than the obvious changes in buildings and styles. They, like many other resorts, are so clearly the result of particular historical circumstances. And yet how strange it all seems: that through thick and thin, the English holiday-maker should return time and again to the places where his forefathers found such unique pleasures – beside the seaside.

Bibliography and Guide to Further Reading

Chapter 1. *Taking the Waters*

ASPIN, C. *Lancashire, the First Industrial Society*, Helmshore Historical Society, 1969.

AYTON, R. *A Voyage Round Great Britain, Undertaken in the Summer of the Year* 1813, 1814.

BAGWELL, P. S. *The Transport Revolution from 1770*, London, 1974.

BAILEY, F. A. 'The Origin and Growth of Southport', *The Town Planning Review*, vol. XXI (1950).

BAKER, J. A. *The History of Scarborough from the Earliest Date*, London, 1882.

BARKER, T. C. and ROBBINS, M. *A History of London Transport*, vol. II, London, 1974.

BRAND, J. *Observations on the Popular Antiquities of Great Britain*, 3 vols., London, 1848.

BROCKFIELD, H. C. 'Worthing: a study of a modern coastal town', *The Town Planning Review*, vol. XXIII (1952–3).

BROWN, A. F. J. *Essex People, 1750–1900*, Essex Record Office, 1970. *The Diary of Fanny Burney*, London, 1940 edition.

DARBY, H. C. *A New Historical Geography of England*, Cambridge, 1973.

EARDLEY, S. *The Lord's Day; is it a holy day or a holiday*, Birmingham, 1838.

GEORGE, M. D. *Hogarth to Cruickshank: Social Change in Graphic Satire*, London, 1967.

GILBERT, E. W. 'The Growth of Inland and Seaside Health Resorts in England', *Scottish Geographical Magazine*, vol. 55 (1939).

——. 'The Growth of Brighton', *Geographical Journal*, vol. 114 (1949).

——. *Brighton: Old Ocean's Bauble*, London, 1954.

——. 'The Holiday Industry and Seaside Towns in England and Wales', *Festschrift Leopold G. Scheidl zum 60 Geburtstag*, vol. I, Vienna, 1965.

GRANVILLE, A. B. *Spas of England*, 1841, 2 vols., 1971 edition.

HIBBERT, C. *George IV*, Harmondsworth, 1976.

HINDERWELL, T. *The History and Antiquities of Scarborough and the Vicinity*, 1798.

HOSKINS, W. G. *Devon*, London, 1954.

Household Tracts for the People, London, 1863.

HUTTON, T. *A Tour to Scarborough in* 1803, second edition, 1817.

LAVER, J. *Victorian Vista*, London, 1954.

LENNARD, R. 'The Watering Places', in R. Lennard (ed.), *Englishmen at Rest and Play*, Oxford, 1931.

LEWIS, S. *A Topographical Dictionary of England*, 5 vols., London, 1831.

MALCOLMSON, R. W. *Popular Recreation in English Society, 1700–1850*, Cambridge, 1973.

MILLWARD, R. *Lancashire. An Illustrated Essay in the History of the Landscape*, London, 1955.

MUSGRAVE, C. *Life at Brighton*, London, 1970.

Railroadiana, London, 1838.

Remarks on the Regulation of Railway Travelling on Sundays . . . by a Railway Director, London, 1836.

RODGERS, E. C. *Discussion of Holidays in the Late Middle Ages*, New York, 1940.

ROWNTREE, A. (ed.) *The History of Scarborough*, London, 1931.

RUSSELL, DR RICHARD. *A Dissertation on the Use of Sea-Water in the Diseases of the Glands*, London, 1752.

Schofield's Guide to Scarborough, second edition, 1796.

STRUTT, JOSEPH. *The Sports and Pastimes of the People of England*, 1801.

WITTIE, R. *Scarborough Spaw*, 1660.

Chapter 2. *The Coming of the Railways*

BARKER, T. C. and HARRIS, J. R. *A Merseyside Town in the Industrial Revolution: St Helens, 1750–1900*, London, 1959.

BRIDGES, J. *The Sabbath Railway System Practically Discussed*, London, 1847.

BROOKE, D. 'Opposition to Sunday Rail Services in North East England, 1834–1914', *Journal of Transport History*, vol. VI, no. 2 (1963).

BURROWS, J. W. *Southend-on-Sea and District: Historical Notes*, Southend-on-Sea, 1909.

CARTER, E. F. *A Historical Geography of the Railways of the British Isles*, London, 1959.

Census for 1851, *Parliamentary Papers*, vol. LXXXV (1852–3).

COLE, M. 'The Growth of the Tourist Industry in Rhyl', unpublished thesis, Crewe and Alsager Colleges, 1974.

DAYSH, G. H. J. (ed.) *A Survey of Whitby and Surrounding Area*, Oxford, 1958.

HAMMOND, J. L. and B. *The Age of the Chartists, 1832–54*, London, 1930.

HONIBORNE, T. *A Tract for Early Closing . . .*, London, 1843.

INGLIS, K. G. *Churches and the Working Classes in Victorian England*, London, 1963.

MANDERS, F. W. *A History of Gateshead*, Gateshead Corporation, 1973.

MANNERS, LORD JOHN. M.P. *A Plea for National Holy Days*, second edition, 1843.

MARCHANT, R. 'Early Excursion Trains', *Railway Magazine*, 100 (1954).

MYERSCOUGH, J. 'Thomas Cook', *Eminently Victorian*, B.B.C. Publications, 1974.

OTLEY, G. *A Bibliography of British Railway History*, London, 1965.

PERKIN, H. *The Age of the Railways*, London, 1970 edition.

'The Pleasure of Piers', *The Architects' Journal*, 24 September 1975.

POLLARD, S. *A History of Labour in Sheffield*, Liverpool, 1959.

'The Saturday Early Closing Movement', *Punch*, vol. XXVI (1854).

THOMAS, D. ST JOHN. *Regional History of the Railways of Great Britain*, vol. I; The West Country, London, 1960.

WILLIAMS, B. 'Piers Closed. An Account of the Development of the Pleasure Piers; Their Decline and Future Prospects', unpublished thesis, Institute of Architectural Studies, University of York, 1974.

Chapter 3. *Work, Rest and Play*

AMBROSE, P. *The Quiet Revolution: Social Change in a Sussex Village*, Sussex University Press, 1974.

AVEBURY, LORD. *Essays and Addresses, 1900–1903*, London, 1903.

BLACK, E. C. *Victorian Culture and Society*, New York, 1973.

BOOTH, CHARLES. *Life and Labour*, final volume, London, 1903.

BOOTH, WILLIAM. *In Darkest England and the Way Out*, London, 1890.

BROOK SMITH, M. *The Growth and Development of Popular Pastimes in the Lancashire Cotton Towns, 1830–70*, M.Litt. thesis, Lancaster University, 1970.

BURNETT, J. (ed.) *Useful Toil*, London, 1974.

CHAMBERS, J. D. *The Workshop of the World*, London, 1968 edition.

COURT, W. H. B. *British Economic History, 1870–1914*, Cambridge, 1965.

DUFF, A. G. (ed.) *The Life and Work of Lord Avebury*, London, 1924.

GROSSMITH, G. and W. *The Diary of a Nobody*, 1892, Harmondsworth, 1975.

HUTCHINSON, H. G. *Life of Sir John Lubbock*, 2 vols., London, 1914.

INGESTRE, VISCOUNT. (ed.) *Meliora, or Better Times to Come*, 1971 edition.

MANDLE, W. F. 'Games People Played', *Historical Studies*, 15 April 1973.

MILLER, W. *Our English Shores*, London, 1888.

MOLYNEUX, D. D. *The Development of Physical Recreation in the Birmingham District, 1871–92*, M.A. thesis, University of Birmingham, 1957.

PIMLOTT, J. A. R. *The Englishman's Holiday*, London, 1947, 1976 edition.

POLLARD, S. and CROSSLEY, D. W. *The Wealth of Britain*, London, 1968.

REES, R. *The Development of Physical Education in Liverpool During the 19th Century*, M.A. thesis, Liverpool University, 1968.

ROWNTREE, S. *Poverty: A Study of Town Life*, London, 1903.

The Saturday Half Holiday Guide, London, 1868.

Saturday Half Holidays, London, 1856.

The Saturday Half Holiday Question at Oldham, 1872.

The Times, 2 June, 3 June, 1865.

WEBB, B. and S. *Industrial Democracy*, London, 1920 edition.

WEBB, S. and COX, H. *The Eight Hour Day*, London, 1891.

(WRIGHT, THOMAS). A Journeyman Engineer. *The Great Unwashed*, London, 1868, 1970 edition.

Chapter 4. *Life at the Seaside*

ADBURGHAM, A. *A Punch History of Manners and Modes, 1841–1940*, London, 1961.

——. *Shops and Shopping, 1800–1914*, London, 1964.

ALEXANDER, W. *On the Seabathing of Scarborough*, Halifax, 1882.

At the Seaside, 4 vols., London, 1884.

BAILEY, F. A. *A History of Southport*, Southport, 1955.

Blackpool, Paris and Sodom, Blackpool, 1896.

Black's Picturesque Guide to Scarborough, Edinburgh, 1862.

CRAVEN, A. B. *Victorian and Edwardian Yorkshire from Old Photographs*, London, 1971.

CUNNINGHAM, P. and MANSFIELD, A. *English Costumes for Sports and Outdoor Recreation*, London, 1969.

DOYLE, R. *Bird's Eye View of Society*, London, 1864.

DUBOS, R. and J. *The White Plague*, London, 1953.

GASKIN, R. T. *The Old Seaport of Whitby*, Whitby, 1909.

GELL, SIR W. *Handbook for the Vale of Clwyd*, 1851.

GOODRICKE, F. *Scarborough and Scarborough Spa*, London, 1891.

HONRI, P. *Working the Halls*, London, 1974.

HOWE, G. M. *Man, Environment and Disease in Britain*, Newton Abbot, 1972.

HYDE, J. 'Blackpool of Today', *Windsor Magazine*, 1896.

MATHIAS, P. *Retailing Revolution*, London, 1967.

PERKIN, H. 'The "Social Tone" of Victorian Seaside Resorts in the North West', *Northern History*, vol. 11 (1975–6).

PRIESTLAND, G. *Frying Tonight: The Saga of Fish and Chips*, London, 1972.

QUENNELL, M. and C. H. B. *A History of Everyday Things in England, 1851–1914*, London, 1958.

ROSE, CLARKSON. *Beside the Seaside*, London, 1960.

Seaside Library, London, 1887.

Seaside Library, London, 1897.

Seaside Musings, London, 1872.
Seaside Packet, London, 1878.
Seaside Sketches, London, 1890.
Seaside Stories, London, 1904.
Seaside Watering Places, London, 1876.
SINGER, C. and UNDERWOOD, E. A. *A Short History of Medicine*, Oxford, 1962.
(STEPHEN, LESLIE). 'Vacations by a Cynic', *Cornhill Magazine*, vol. 20, no. 116 (August 1869).
THOMPSON, P. *The Edwardians*, London, 1975.
The Times, 30 August 1860.
WALTON, JOHN. 'Residential Amenity: Respectable Morality and the Rise of the Entertainment Industry in Blackpool', *Literature and History*, no. 1 (March 1975).
WILSON, C. *Economic History and the Historian*, London, 1968.
YEO, J. B. *Health Resorts and Their Uses*, London, 1882.
——. 'On Change of Air', *Nineteenth Century*, 26, 1889.
YONGE, C. M. 'Victorians by the Sea', *History Today*, September 1975.

Chapter 5. *Into a New Century*

Blackpool Guide, 1906.
BRIGGS, A. *Social Thought and Social Action: A Study of the Work of Seebohm Rowntree*, London, 1961.
CHURCHILL, W. S. *My Early Life*, London, 1970 edition.
DEAN OF MANCHESTER. 'The True Holiday', *The British Review*, August 1913.
HOBSBAWM, E. J. *Industry and Empire*, London, 1968.
KEATING, P. (ed.) *Into Unknown England*, London, 1976.
KYNASTON, D. *King Labour: The British Working Class, 1850–1914*, London, 1976.
LANCASTER, O. *All Done from Memory*, London, 1953.
LEIGHTON, CLARE. 'The annual exodus', in M. E. Edes and D. Fraser (eds.), *The Age of Extravagance*, London, 1955.
LLOYD, T. O. *Empire to Welfare State*, Oxford, 1970.
MCCARTHY, G. 'Holidays, Poverty and Human Life', *The British Review*, August 1913.
MASTERMAN, C. F. G. *The Condition of England*, London, 1909.
MILLS, C. M. *Vacations for Industrial Workers*, New York, 1927.
MUSSON. A. E. *Enterprise in Soap and Chemicals*, Manchester, 1965.
PATMORE, J. A. *Land and Leisure*, Newton Abbot, 1970.
ROBERTS, R. *The Classic Slum*, Harmondsworth, 1973.
Seaside Diary, 1903.
Seaside Fun, 1902.
Seaside Pictures and Stories, London, 1908.
Seaside Stories, 3 vols., London, 1904.
WALTON, J. K. *The Social Development of Blackpool, 1788–1914*, Ph.D. thesis, Lancaster University, 1974.
WOOD, REV. T. *What We Found at the Seaside*, London, 1913.

YOUNG, K. *Music's Great Days in the Spas and Watering Places*, London, 1968.

Chapter 6. *Between the Wars*

ADSHEAD, S. D. *The Further Development of Scarborough*, London, 1938.
ALDERSON, F. *The Comic Postcard and English Life*, Newton Abbot, 1970.
Blackpool Gazetteer and Herald, 'Air Pageant Souvenir', July 1928; 'Supplement', April 1933.
BROCKFIELD, H. C. 'Worthing: A Study of a Modern Coastal Town', *The Town Planning Review*, vol. XXIII (1952–3).
BRUNNER, E. *Holiday Making and the Holiday Trades*, Oxford, 1945.
CHILDS, W. M. *Holidays in Tents*, London, 1921.
Conference on Workers' Holidays, Industrial Welfare Society, London, 1938.
DOUGILL, W. 'The British Coast and its Holiday Resorts', *The Town Planning Review*, vol. XVI, no. 4 (December 1935).
GARLAND, M. *The Indecisive Decade*, London, 1968.
GRAVES, R. and HODGE, A. *The Long Weekend*, London, 1961 edition.
HIBBS, J. (ed.) *The Omnibus*, Newton Abbot, 1971.
Holiday Savings, Industrial Welfare Society, London, 1938.
Holidays with Pay, Ministry of Labour, 1939.
HOLT, T. and V. *Postcards of the Golden Age*, London, 1971.
'Leisure as an Architectural Problem', *Architecture Review*, December 1938.
MARWICK, A. *Britain in the Century of Total War*, Harmondsworth, 1970.
Minutes of Evidence Before the Committee on Holidays with Pay, H.M.S.O., 1937.
MOWAT, C. LOCH. *Britain Between the Wars*, London, 1959.
New Survey of London Life and Labour, vol. IX, London, 1935.
OGILVIE, F. W. *The Tourist Movement*, London, 1933.
ORWELL, G. 'The Art of Donald McGill', *Collected Essays of George Orwell*, vol. 2, Harmondsworth, 1970.
Recreation in Industry, Industrial Welfare Society, London, 1938.
'Report of the Committee on Holidays with Pay', April 1938, Cmnd 5724, *Parliamentary Papers*, vol. XII (1937–8).
ROBERTS, R. *A Ragged Schooling*, Manchester, 1976.
RUST, F. *Dance in Society*, London, 1969.
Scarborough Mercury, 21 October 1938; 28 April 1939.
Southport for a Wintertime Holiday, Southport, 1935.
Sunny Southport for Golden Holiday Hours, Southport, 1936.
STRONG, L. A. G. *The Rolling Road: The Story of Travel*, London, 1956.
TAYLOR, V. *Reminiscences of a Showman*, London, 1971.

Chapter 7. *From Austerity to Prosperity*

BIRCH, J. R. *The Isle of Man: A Study in Economic Geography*, Cambridge, 1964.

BLOCH, G. B. M. *Britons on Holiday*, London, 1963.

DIXON, P. A. *The Evolution of Scarborough*, B.A. thesis, Liverpool University, 1965.

EYRE, K. *Seven Golden Miles*, Lytham, 1961.

Gerrard Young Collection, Bognor Regis College of Education.

HOLFORD, W. 'The Future of Spa and Resort Towns', *Journal of the Town Planning Institute*, June 1955.

Hours and Holidays, Labour Party Research Dept, London, 1974.

PATMORE, J. A. *Land and Leisure*, Newton Abbot, 1970.

PEARSON, R. E. *The Lincolnshire Coast Holiday Region*, M.A. thesis, Nottingham University, 1965.

ROWNTREE, S. and LAVERS, G. R. *English Life and Leisure*, London, 1951.

Seebohm Rowntree Papers, Borthwick Institute, York.

For U.S. Armed Forces in the U.K., Southport, 1943.

Chapter 8. *More Prosperous Times*

ADSHEAD, S. D. *The Future Development of Scarborough*, London, 1938.

Board of Trade. White Paper, *Staggered Holidays*, Cmnd 2105, July 1963.

British Tourist Authority. *Research Newsletter*, no. 13, summer 1974.

——. *Digest of Tourist Statistics*, no. 5, April 1975.

HALSEY, A. H. *Trends in British Society Since 1900*, London, 1972.

JAMIESON and MACKENZIE. *Blackpool Transportation Study*, 1972.

LANE, L. *Planning for Leisure in Britain*, London, 1968.

LAVEY, P. *Recreational Geography*, Newton Abbot, 1974.

LICKORISH, L. J. and KERSHAW, A. G. *The Travel Trade*, London, 1958.

Report of the Regional Planning Committee for the Area of the Fylde, London, 1937.

SMITH, M. A., PARKER, S. R. and SMITH, C. S. *Leisure and Society in Britain*, London, 1973.

Society of Town Clerks. *Annual Meeting*, Blackpool, 1939.

STUDD, R. G. *The Holiday Story*, London, 1958.

TURNBULL, P. 'Planning for the Holiday Maker', *Journal of the Town Planning Institute*, vol. XLVIII, no. 7 (1962).

Index